Three American Modernist Painters

Max Weber
with an introduction by Alfred H. Barr, Jr.

Maurice Sterne
by H. M. Kallen, with a note by the artist

Stuart Davis
by James Johnson Sweeney

The Museum of Modern Art, New York
Reprint Edition, 1969
Published for The Museum of Modern Art by Arno Press

Copyright © 1933, 1945 by
The Museum of Modern Art, New York
Reprint Edition, 1969 Arno Press
Library of Congress Catalog Card No. 70-86440

MAX WEBER

JANUARY 1930

MAX WEBER

RETROSPECTIVE EXHIBITION

1907   1930

MARCH 13   1930   APRIL 2

MUSEUM OF MODERN ART

730 FIFTH AVENUE   NEW YORK

ACKNOWLEDGMENT

The exhibition has been selected from the following collections:

DOCTOR F. H. HIRSCHLAND, NEW YORK

MR. AND MRS. SAMUEL A. LEWISOHN, NEW YORK

MRS. NATHAN J. MILLER, NEW ROCHELLE, NEW YORK

MR. J. B. NEUMANN, NEW YORK

Mr. JULIUS OPPENHEIMER, NEW YORK

MRS. JOHN D. ROCKEFELLER. JR., NEW YORK

MR. ALBERT ROTHBART, NEW YORK

DR. B. D. SAKLATWALLA, CRAFTON, PENNSYLVANIA

NEWARK MUSEUM ASSOCIATION, NEWARK

PHILLIPS MEMORIAL GALLERY, WASHINGTON

In addition to those who have lent pictures the Trustees and the staff wish to thank Mrs. Edith Gregor Halpert of the Downtown Gallery for her generous co-operation in assembling a part of the exhibition.

TRUSTEES

INTRODUCTION *

It is difficult to write briefly of Max Weber. His spirit shines with a grave simplicity. But his mind is complexly furnished with an intimate knowledge of the art of our day and of past and exotic periods; the development of his style is a compendium of the problems of early twentieth century painting; and his career is rich in contacts with the important artistic personalities of the last three decades in France and in America.

As a boy he brought with him to New York the memories of his childhood in Russia where both Slav and Jew had still preserved what is so lacking in America, a racial culture of authentic purity and color. After graduation from a Brooklyn High School he was most fortunate in choosing the Pratt Institute where Arthur Wesley Dow taught the theory and practice of design. No one else in America during the nineties emphasized so exclusively a formal attitude toward painting and no one else combined such a stimulating knowledge of Far Eastern aesthetics with the not dissimilar principles which were then emerging in France. For Dow had worked both with Fenelosa in Boston and in 1889 with Gauguin at Pont-Aven. Dow's intelligent instruction made a lasting impression upon his young pupil who was, however, to pass far beyond his master's somewhat limited theories of two dimensional design.

While at the Pratt Institute Weber also studied joinery and mastered academic drawing so that he acquired a thorough respect for fine craftsmanship. So facile did he become from an academic point-of-view that he had no difficulty in obtaining several teaching positions and finally at the age of twenty-one the Chairmanship of the Art Department at the Michigan State Normal School.

By 1905 he had earned enough money to pay his way to Paris where he stayed through 1908. These three years gave birth to events of supreme importance in progressive modern painting. During 1906 and 1907 Cézanne's art was revealed to the younger painters in a series of great exhibitions. At the same time and partially as a result of the Cézanne exhibitions the *fauves* group, the "Wild Beasts"—Matisse, Derain, Vlaminck, Friesz, Rouault—was organized as a body of shock troops against the academic art of the period as well as against the already degenerate Impressionist and Synthetist movements. During 1907 and '08 Picasso and Braque were also studying Cézanne's art and were adding to these researches certain principles of design which they had discovered in negro sculpture.

* The writer wishes to thank MR. HOLGER CAHILL for much of the information included in these notes. A book on Max Weber by MR. CAHILL is about to be published.

Weber was witness of and frequently participant in these stirring activities. Many of the new ideas had been implicit in the teaching of Dow but he now found them realized with compelling power in the work of Matisse and Picasso. The former interested him especially. So much so that after an unsatisfactory period of work under that academic martinet Jean Paul Laurens he helped to form with the Bavarian Hans Purrmann a small class to study under Matisse.

There were other equally important influences upon the young student. He came to know most intimately Henri Rousseau *le douanier*. His naïve vision and ingenuous spirit impressed Weber deeply. More thoroughly than Matisse Weber studied Persian and Indian miniatures and Coptic textiles. More earnestly than Picasso he absorbed not merely the form but something of the spirit of negro sculpture. To this knowedge he added hours spent in the Louvre before the archaic sculpture of Egypt, Assyria and Greece, in the Trocadero before the sculpture of mediaeval France, and in the *Musée Guimet* before the painting and stone figures of China and Japan. Nor did he neglect the great Renaissance and Baroque traditions of European art. Visits to Spain disclosed to him El Greco, Velasquez and Goya. In Italy he studied far more thoroughly than he could in the Louvre the work of Giotto, Castagno, Piero della Francesca, Michelangelo, Titian. He became in short highly educated in the history of art which he understood with a profoundly sensitive intuition. But he was also becoming a painter.

At the end of the year 1908 Weber returned to New York to find that almost no one had heard of his gods Cézanne and Gauguin, much less of his friends Picasso, Derain, Delaunay, Metzinger, and "that angel," Henri Rousseau. In the previous winter Alfred Stieglitz had exhibited at the "291" gallery lithographs and drawings by Matisse to an uncomprehending public. In Baltimore the Misses Cone encouraged by Gertrude Stein had brought over paintings by Matisse as early as 1906. But America as a whole still found Impressionism a matter for controversy.

New York in 1908 was not, however, without its "modernists." The group of "The Eight" had just held a provocative exhibition. They were Robert Henri, George Luks and John Sloan who painted in a manner which Manet had made popular in Europe during the 'seventies, William Glackens, a follower of Renoir, Arthur B. Davies, an eclectic mannerist, Everett Shinn, Ernest Lawson and Maurice Prendergast at that time painting more or less as impressionists. They were painters variously of taste, power and intelligence yet because of their

8

rather mild secession they were dubbed a "revolutionary black gang" and met with excited opposition from the academicians.

Weber's first exhibition was held in April 1909. Those who came laughed or grew angry at what they did not understand. But Arthur Davies bought two of Weber's paintings, his first of many generous gestures of encouragement to an artist who met with little elsewhere. Between 1910 and 1915 Weber held six more one-man shows, twice at "291," at the Montross, and at the Ehrich Galleries. At the Newark Museum John Cotton Dana gave him his first exhibition outside of New York. And in 1913 Roger Fry who had been Curator of Painting at the Metropolitan Museum, invited him to send five paintings to London to exhibit with the Grafton Group. Weber sent eleven so that five might be selected. Fry and his group were so enthusiastic that they exhibited all eleven. Weber and Kandinsky, the other guest exhibitor, bore the brunt of critical attack in London.

In the same year, 1913, was held the great Armory Exhibition where the art which Weber had known in Paris seven years before now baffled and enraged Americans. But most of the critics still retained a few barbs for Weber's exhibitions. A page of quotations from the contemporary press reprinted elsewhere in this catalog gives some idea of the insulting virulence of their attitude.

A few of course protested against the bigoted intolerance to which Weber yearly exposed himself and his work. But in spite of the encouragement of such men as Dana, Fry, Davies and Henri, and the courageous patronage of Mrs. Nathan J. Miller, his sensitive nature became weary of the ceaseless unequal struggle. Between 1916 and 1923 he exhibited only occasional pictures. But during this period he produced some of his finest and certainly his most personal work, colored though much of it was by discouragement and distress both economic and spiritual.

In 1923 he returned to the world with an exhibition at Montross and in the five succeeding years with four exhibitions at J. B. Neumann's New Art Circle. Partial success rewarded him. Several critics now supported him staunchly, especially Mr. Henry McBride who asserted that Weber was one of the half dozen finest living painters. A few far-seeing collectors bought his work but most of his paintings went back to his studio unpurchased and by the "art-loving" public practically unseen. Even today after twenty years of exhibiting his uncompromising art is very far from popular.

Weber's art can best be studied in the present exhibition by concentrating on a few characteristic examples. At the risk of destruction by future historians these four divisions of his development are suggested.

1905 to 1908 The Student Period in Paris
1909 to 1917 The Period of Experiment
1918   Introspection and Self-discovery
1919 to —   The Period of Maturity

PERIOD I. 1905–1908. THE STUDENT IN PARIS

The Young Model, 1907, (No. 2) painted in pale tonalities, flat modelling, simplified contours. The feeling for pattern suggests the teaching of Dow and the study of Oriental art to which homage is paid by the print on the wall behind the model.

Figure Study, 1908, (No. 6). The vigor of this sketch made from the model in Matisse's studio is remarkable when contrasted with the flaccid drawing and rather insipid color of the previous year.

PERIOD II. 1909–1917. EXPERIMENT

Weber brought back with him to New York ideas which he had not had time to realize in Paris. *Summer*, 1909, (No. 8) is a typical *fauve* painting, emphatic in design, bold in color with blocky simplified masses and heavy outlines. Derain and Friesz were working along similar lines in Paris. In *Composition with Three Figures*, 1910, (No. 12) the figures are more arbitrarily simplified than in *Summer*. The flat planes and sharp edges suggest the technique of negro sculpture. The composition is compressed and dense, very different from the baroque spaciousness of *Summer*. *Drawing for Carving* (No. 17), also of 1910, reflects Weber's studies in Alaskan and pre-Columbian art at the American Museum of Natural History.

Breakfast, 1911, (No. 18) suggests research into the flat arabesque design of Oriental miniatures and textiles.

The Geranium (No. 19), the most important painting of 1911, is well analyzed by Mr. Weber as an experiment in "crystalizing" form, that is, breaking the surfaces and contours into facets. The angular composition, the nervous tension of the drawing, the sumptuous blue color accented by the geranium are of a quality nowhere equalled in Weber's previous work.

Between 1912 and 1914 Weber experimented with a series of compositions in which flat simplified shapes were adjusted with great precision. *Four Sails*, 1912, (No. 24) is perhaps the finest in the group though *Decoration with a Cloud*, 1913, (No. 27) is more imposing. *Maine*, 1914, (No. 31) reduces the seacoast most interestingly to an arrangement of geometric symbols suggestive of Egyptian or American Indian painting.

Between 1913 and 1915 are several paintings employing some of the technical devices of the Italian futurists. *Rush Hour, New York*, 1915, (No. 33) is a kinetograph of the flickering shutters of speed through subways and under skyscrapers. *Chinese Restaurant*, 1915, (No. 34) in a similar technique is admirably described by Mr. Weber himself.

The elementary phase of cubism illustrated several years previously by the *Composition with Three Figures* (No. 12) and *Two Heads* (No. 25) is developed between 1913 and 1917. *Imaginary Portrait of a Woman* (No. 28) was the center of bitter argument in 1913 when it was first shown. The head is drawn partially full-face, partially in profile, thus creating a special problem in design. It should be compared technically with the figures in the *Geranium* (No. 19) of two years earlier. *The Woman* is static and monumental in mood, the *Geranium* dramatic and dynamic. More abstract are *Avoirdupois* (No. 36), *The Piqué Shirt* (No. 39) and *The Cellist* (No. 45), all three of which are discussed by Mr. Weber in the catalog list. A number of small gouaches and pastels form a delightful series of improvisations in the cubistic technique (e.g. Nos. 41, 42, 51, 52, 53).

During this period of experiment Weber painted several purely abstract compositions. Very different are *Interior with Music* (No. 32) and *New York at Night* (No. 35) both of 1915, the former a study in easy swinging curves, the latter in staccato angles and sharp contrasts in color.

PERIOD III. 1918. INTROSPECTION AND SELF-DISCOVERY

The year 1918 seems to be a turning point in Weber's art. Most of his earlier work is sufficiently informed by Weber's spirit to make his experiments whether *fauve*, cubist, or futurist peculiarly his own. But in 1918 he seems first to have discovered a *style* which is unmistakably "Weber" and in so doing produced two series of designs which are surely among the most remarkable in American art. These are the series of small gouaches some four or five inches square (Nos. 57 to 62 inclusive) of which about fifty exist and a series of some thirty woodcuts (Nos. 64 to 73 inclusive), frequently printed in color. In these tiny compositions Weber seems to have found himself completely. Their jewel-like color and their depth of sentiment are most rare. The mood of contemplative melancholy which frequently invests them appears also in larger paintings of the same year such as *The Musicians* (No. 51). A poignant ecstacy envelopes *The Sisters* (No. 48), a religious mood of mystical purity is suggested in *The Rabbi* (No. 49) and *The Worshipper* (No. 50).

PERIOD IV. SINCE 1918. MATURITY

The extraordinary intimacy and depth of feeling of the year 1918 is transformed in the following years into a more objective and monumental style in which figure composition and still life rival each other to the accompaniment of an occasional landscape. In *Invocation*, 1919, (No. 74) the religious mood of the previous year is dramatized and externalized into a powerful monumental composition. More three-dimensional in arrangement is the *Figures as Architecture* (No. 81) of 1922 in which the figure-motives are buttressed and counter-buttressed. Of especial beauty is the frieze of *Eight Figures*, 1927, (No. 89), symmetrical but varied as subtly as the reliefs of a Greek sarcophagus or a design by Pollaiuolo. *Tranquility*, 1930, (No. 98) the most recent of these compositions is remarkable for its ease and grandeur of gesture and its sense of repose.

Upon apples and jugs Weber has spent some of his finest painting. In the *Blue Saucer*, 1926, (No. 85) and the *Still Life, Distributed*, 1929, (No. 94) Weber dares to challenge Cézanne. And if he fails to win the bout, what other living painter would fare better?

But it is scarcely by his still life paintings or by the drenched blue of his landscapes that Weber most clearly commands our study, nor by any external or purely aesthetic quality of paint or of arrangement; it is rather by the penetrating, pathetic sentiment of his more intimate and personal compositions—by a quality of spirit.

A. H. B., JR.

CHRONOLOGY

1881	Born in Byalostok, Russia.
1891	To America with parents, settling in Brooklyn.
1897	Graduated from the Boys' High School, Brooklyn.
1897–1900	Studied at Pratt Institute under Arthur Wesley Dow.
1900–05	Taught drawing and painting in public schools, Lynchburg, Virginia; summer school, University of Virginia; State Normal School, Duluth, Michigan.
1905	To Paris. Studied at the Julian Academy under Jean Paul Laurens, and independently at the Colarossi Academy and the Academy of the *Grande Chaumière*. Frequent visits to the Louvre, the Trocadero, and the Guimet Museum of Oriental Art.
1906	To Spain in the summer: El Greco, Velasquez, and Goya. Exhibited *Salon des Indépendents* and *Salon d'Automne*. Met Henri Rousseau, Flandrin, Matisse, Marquet, Picasso, Delaunay, Gleizes, Guillaume Apollinaire.
1907	To Italy: Giotto, Masaccio, Piero della Francesca, Donatello, and the masters of the High Renaissance. Back to Paris to study with Matisse. Great Cézanne exhibition at the *Petit Palais*. Exhibited at both advanced salons.
1908	Paris. First notice in America, New York Times, October 11th, 1908, mentioning his exhibiting in the Salon "several pictures of an ultra-modern variety" one of which was hung upside down.
1909	Returned to New York. First one man show at the Haas Gallery, in April. Two paintings purchased by Arthur B. Davies.
1910	March: Exhibited at the "291" Gallery (Alfred Stieglitz) with Marin, Maurer, Hartley, and Dove. September: Arranged first American exhibition of paintings by Henri Rousseau at "291." Visited continually American Museum of Natural History, ethnographical section.
1911	One man show at "291," "a brutal, vulgar, and unnecessary display."
1912	One man show, Murray Hill Galleries.
1913	*Cubist Poems* published in London. March: At the invitation of Roger Fry exhibited at the Alpine Club Gallery, London, with the Grafton group (Vanessa Bell, Duncan Grant, Wyndham Lewis, Roger Fry, Frederick Etchells; Kandinsky the only other foreign exhibitor).

June: One man show at the Newark Museum, organized by John Cotton Dana.

1914–18　Lectured on history and appreciation of art at the White School of Photography.

1915　Retrospective exhibitions at the Ehrich and Montross galleries.

1916　*Essays on Art* published. Did not exhibit again until 1923 (except occasional paintings in general exhibitions).

1920–21　Taught at the Art Students' League.

1923　One man show at the Montross gallery.

1924, 1925　One man shows, J. B. Neumann gallery.

1926　*Primitives* (a second book of poems) published. Taught again at the Art Students' League.

1927, 1928　One man shows, J. B. Neumann Gallery.

1929　Exhibited Museum of Modern Art, "Nineteen Living Americans."

TWENTY YEARS AGO

The following quotations are excerpts from criticisms of Weber's exhibitions between 1910 and 1912.

Weber Exhibition, "291" Gallery, January, 1911

"Here are travesties of the human form—that seem for all the world like emanations such as one might expect from the inmate of a lunatic asylum.—It is difficult to write of these atrocities with moderation, for they are positively an insult to ordinary intelligence."

New York Globe, January 17, 1911

"No one is going to believe that nature alone ever made anybody so bad an artist as all this. Such grotesquerie can only be acquired by long and perverse practice."

New York Evening World, January 18, 1911

"This exhibition as the first show of an ambitious young painter with a firm belief in his own mission is worthy of attention and study."　New York Herald, January 11, 1911

"A future generation may call this Art but the present writer cannot conscientiously give it that term."　American Art News, January 11, 1911

"It is really too much to ask the open-minded critic to look upon this as art."

Cincinnati Times Star, January 28, 1911

Weber Exhibition, Murray Hill Galleries, February, 1912

"—distorted notions of art requirements, ugly color, hopelessly stupid drawing and absurd compositions."　New York Globe, February, 1912

CATALOG

The pictures are arranged in chronological order regardless of medium. An asterisk before a number indicates that the picture is illustrated by the half-tone reproduction bearing the same number. Mr. Weber has written the notes signed by his initials, M. W. The pictures are from the collection of the artist unless otherwise noted.

1 PARIS, 1907
Oil on canvas, 24¾ x 31 inches

*2 THE YOUNG MODEL, 1907
Oil on canvas, 38½ x 31½ inches

3 FIGURE, 1907
Pencil, 13¼ x 8¼ inches

4 SKETCH, 1907
Charcoal, 12 x 6¼ inches

5 ON THE SHORE, 1907
Ink, 9 x 12 inches

6 FIGURE STUDY, 1908
Oil on canvas-board, 22 x 12 inches
> NOTE: This study was made from the model in Matisse's class. Complementary colors of green-yellow and red-violet are used. Matisse admired this study, especially the drawing of the legs. He always encouraged directness and simplification in the indication of contour and mass.

7 STUDY FROM MODEL, 1908
Pencil, 6¾ x 4½ inches

8 SUMMER, 1909
Oil on canvas, 39¾ x 23¾ inches

9 STILL LIFE WITH BANANAS, 1909
Oil on canvas, 32 x 25½ inches

10 STATUETTE, 1909
Pencil and watercolor, 10 x 6¾ inches

11 THE OLD AMERICAN ART GALLERIES, 1909
Gouache, 9¼ x 6½ inches

*12 COMPOSITION WITH THREE FIGURES, 1910
Oil on corrugated paper, 47 x 23½ inches

13 BOY, 1910
Gouache, 28½ x 12 inches

14 MEDALLION, 1910
Watercolor, oval, 5 x 4 inches

15 RED PARASOL, 1910
Watercolor, 7⅛ x 4⅝ inches

16 FIGURE—SIDE VIEW, 1910
Charcoal and chalk, 9½ x 3½ inches

17 DRAWING FOR CARVING, 1910
Pencil, 12½ x 8 inches

18 BREAKFAST, 1911
Pastel and gouache on corrugated paper, 47½ x 23¾ inches

*19 THE GERANIUM, 1911
Oil on canvas, 39¼ x 31¾ inches
        NOTE: Two crouching figures of women dwelling and brooding in a nether or unworldly realm.
        The conception and treatment spring from a search of form in the crystal. It is a painter's realiza-
        tion of sculpturesque and tactile values.—M. W.

20 TWO FIGURES, 1911, Study for The Geranium
Oil on canvas-board, 12 x 17¾ inches

21 THE BLACK FENCE, 1911
Oil on canvas-board, 15¼ x 17¼ inches

22 FIGURE COMPOSITION, 1911
Watercolor, 18 x 24½ inches

23 FIGURE STUDY, 1911
Ink and gouache, 11½ x 6 inches

24 FOUR SAILS, 1912
Oil on canvas, 35½ x 20½ inches

25 TWO HEADS, 1912
Pastel, 24¼ x 18 inches

26 FIGURE, 1912
Gouache, 15 x 10¾ inches

*27 DECORATION WITH CLOUD, 1913
Oil on canvas, 59¼ x 40 inches
        NOTE: A few simple objects—a black tree, white blossoms, a portion of a hut with a carmine
        colored roof, a pale yellowish green cloud, birds, two figures of primitive type in attitudes of
        gaze and quest—are placed with utmost regard for distribution and space, and beauty of

design and color. This is purely decorative study, arabesque and primitive in its intent. Charm or sweetness was avoided. Flat, subdued, intermediary tints were chosen in a manner that seemed to help in mellowing the expression of primitive austerity.—M. W.

28 IMAGINARY PORTRAIT OF A WOMAN, 1913
Oil on canvas, 35½ x 24¼ inches
Collection Mrs. Nathan J. Miller, New Rochelle, New York

29 WOMEN AND TENTS, 1913
Oil on canvas, 24½ x 35¾ inches
Collection Mrs. Nathan J. Miller, New Rochelle, New York

30 THE BATHER, 1913
Oil on canvas, 59½ x 23½ inches

*31 MAINE, 1914
Pastel, 24½ x 18 inches

32 INTERIOR WITH MUSIC, 1915
Oil on canvas, 59¼ x 40 inches
NOTE: There are moments when our senses seem to take on the functions of each other. To hear is to see, to see is to touch, and so it seems that the audible tones of music float and interlace or blur in space as do volumes of smoke or even vapors or aromas. Here is an expression of a conception of music as it wafts in space and is encased or seized in rhythmic architectural contour. The visible gamut of color seemed appropriate at the time for the harmony of music then heard in silence and isolation.—M. W.

33 RUSH HOUR, NEW YORK, 1915
Oil on canvas, 35¾ x 29½ inches

34 CHINESE RESTAURANT, 1915
Oil on canvas, 39½ x 47½ inches
NOTE: On entering a Chinese Restaurant from the darkness of the night outside, a maze and blaze of light seemed to split into fragments the interior and its contents, the human and inanimate. For the time being the static became transient and fugitive—oblique planes and contours took vertical and horizontal positions, and the horizontal and vertical became oblique, the light so piercing and so luminous, the color so liquid and the life and movement so enchanting! To express this, kaleidoscopic means had to be chosen. The memory of bits of pattern were less obvious than the spirit and festive loveliness and gaiety—almost exotic movement. Therefore, the glow, the charm, the poetry of geometry was stressed. The whole picture is made even more significant by the distribution of flickers here and there in fitting place of a hand, an eye, or drooping head.—M. W.

*35 NEW YORK AT NIGHT, 1915
Oil on canvas, 34 x 22 inches
NOTE: Electrically illumined contours of buildings, rising height upon height against the blackness of the sky now diffused, now interknotted, now pierced by occasional shafts of colored light. Altogether—a web of colored geometric shapes, characteristic only of the Grand Canyons of New York at Night.—M. W.

17

36 AVOIRDUPOIS, 1915
Oil on canvas, 21 x 18 inches

NOTE: Inanimate objects are exceedingly fascinating. A life all their own seems to inform them. The scale, for example, in its process or function of weighing, seems to be a living, balancing, knowing instrument. It searches for equilibrium between matter and matter, regardless of content or composition. It is the moment before the stillness in balance that was aimed at in terms of geometry and symbol.—M. W.

37 COLTS, 1915
Watercolor, 9½ x 13½ inches

38 KITCHEN, 1915
Pastel, 24¼ x 18 inches

*39 THE PIQUÉ SHIRT, 1916
Oil on canvas, 31 x 24 inches

NOTE: Mere caricature was not the aim in this study. It is an effort to express the dignity, poise and concentration of a man seated at a table reading a book. It is a plastic expression of visual memory and not of optic reality.—M. W.

40 WOMAN BATHING, 1917
Gouache, 24¼ x 18 inches

41 COURTING, 1917
Gouache, oval, diameters 24 x 18 inches

*42 LECTURE, METROPOLITAN MUSEUM, 1917
Pastel, 24¼ x 18 inches

NOTE: A lecture on Giotto was given at the Metropolitan Museum. The late hastening visitor finds himself in an interior of plum-colored darkness on leaving the glaring daylight, speed and noise behind. The darkness of the interior becomes a background upon which one discerns the focussing spray-like yellowish-white light, the concentric, circular rows of seats, a portion of the screen, and indications of figures upon it. There was much more visible, but the memory retained only the essential expressed in this pastel study.—M. W.

43 STUDY FOR SCULPTURE, 1917
Pastel, 24 x 15 inches

44 THE FOUNDRY, 1917
Pencil, 5¼ x 7¾ inches

*45 THE CELLIST, 1917
Oil on canvas, 39¾ x 29½ inches

NOTE: Two bearded young French musicians, a cellist and pianist, giving a recital. This is an effort to combine the arabesque with the pictorial. To obtain the unity and rhythm of interlaced form or pattern and the fantastic visual spacial beauty that such interplay evokes, the opaque was treated as if it were transparent, and two or three objects as if they occupied the same space at the same time. The human touch, the spirit and charm of music was cherished and vested in the plastic.—M. W.

46 CONVERSATION, 1917
   Oil on canvas, 41½ x 33½ inches

47 THE EGYPTIAN POT, 1917
   Oil on canvas, 28 x 20 inches
   Collection Mrs. Nathan J. Miller, New Rochelle, New York

*48 THE SISTERS, 1917
   Oil on canvas, 36 x 17¾ inches
      NOTE: This is an expression of withheld emotion or ecstasy—a subconscious state of the spirit.
      Technique, process, style were utterly abandoned and useless in the painting of this picture.
      —M. W.

49 THE RABBI, 1918
   Oil on canvas, 24 x 20 inches
   Collection Mrs. Nathan J. Miller, New Rochelle, New York

50 THE WORSHIPPER, 1918
   Oil on canvas, 30½ x 23¾
   Collection Mrs. Nathan J. Miller, New Rochelle, New York

51 THE MUSICIANS, 1918
   Oil on canvas, 24 x 18 inches
   Collection J. B. Neumann, New York

51a OPPOSITION, 1918
   Gouache, 17 x 11¼ inches

52 SEATED FIGURE, 1918
   Gouache, 8⅛ x 5⅜ inches

53 THE BLACK EYE, 1918
   Gouache, 11¼ x 5⅜ inches

54 INTERSECTION OF SOLIDS—HUMAN, 1918
   Gouache, 8½ x 5¼ inches

55 THE VISIT, 1918
   Gouache, 6 x 12 inches

56 THE BLUE DRESS, 1918
   Gouache, 8¼ x 4½ inches

57 SUPPER, 1918
   Gouache, 4½ x 4½ inches
   Collection J. B. Neumann, New York

58 THE BATH, 1918
Gouache, 4½ x 4½ inches
Collection J. B. Neumann, New York

59 OLD WOMAN IN GREEN CHAIR, 1918
Gouache, 4½ x 4½ inches
Collection J. B. Neumann, New York

*60 THE DRAMATIST, 1918
Gouache, 4½ x 4½ inches
Private Collection, New York

> NOTE: There is a strange scholastic or philosophic affectation or tone about a young aspiring dram-atist or poet. This was particularly obvious in the type portrayed in this little gouache paint-ing. Pale, wan, meditative, sensitive, perhaps a bit morbid, sitting at the table in a leaning posi-tion so natural and peculiar to this type, wandering perhaps in a fourth-dimensional abode. The exaggeration, the grey pearl-like tints seemed fitting and necessary and most appropriate from a plastic viewpoint in the expression, the character and aura of this type.—M. W.

61 THE LEMON, 1918
Gouache, 4¾ x 2¾ inches

62 CRYSTALLINE NUDE, 1918
Gouache, 5 x 3½ inches

63 LANDSCAPE, 1918
Pencil, 5¼ x 7 inches

WOODCUTS, 1918

64 THE WINDOW (No. 17)

65 THOUGHT (No. 30)

66 PRAYER (No. 2)

67 THE BLUE POT (No. 26)

68 MASK WITH A VEIL (No. 5)

69 ABSTRACT HEAD (No. 15)

70 HEAD WITH A CROWN (No. 8)

71 PRIMITIVE MAN (No. 41)

72 ABSTRACT FIGURE (No. 20)

73 MASK WITH TWO BUTTONS (No. 7)

*74 INVOCATION, 1919
Oil on canvas, 48 x 41½ inches

NOTE: Sculpturesque, dynamic form was sought for in this picture, but the chief aim was to express a deep religious archaic spirit in fitting attitudes and gestures.—M. W.

75 THE CAVE, 1920
Ink drawing and watercolor, 9 x 12 inches

76 THE GESTURE, 1921
Oil on canvas, 18 x 22
Collection Dr. F. H. Hirschland, New York

77 THE CUP, 1921
Gouache. 15⅝ x 11¾ inches
Private Collection, New York

78 SEATED FIGURE, 1921
Pencil, 9½ x 6½ inches

79 DAHLIAS AND ZINNIAS, 1922
Oil on canvas, 40 x 18 inches
Collection J. B. Neumann, New York

80 THE BLACK CHAIR, 1922
Oil on canvas, 46½ x 30½ inches

81 FIGURES AS ARCHITECTURE, 1922
Oil on canvas, 20 x 30 inches

82 OUTSKIRTS OF THE TOWN, 1925
Oil on canvas, 21 x 28 inches
Collection Julius Oppenheimer, New York

*83 THE RIVER, 1926
Oil on canvas, 24½ x 29½ inches

84 THE FLUTED BOWL, 1926
Oil on canvas, 39¼ x 31¾ inches
Collection Mrs. Nathan J. Miller, New Rochelle, New York

85 THE BLUE SAUCER, 1926
Oil on canvas, 28 x 23 inches
Collection Mr. and Mrs. Samuel A. Lewisohn, New York

86 RABBI READING, 1926
Oil on canvas, 17½ x 9½ inches
Collection J. B. Neumann, New York

*87 OLD BARNS, 1926
Oil on canvas, 25 x 30 inches
Collection Dr. B. D. Saklatwalla, Crafton, Pennsylvania

88 BOUDOIR, 1926
Gouache, 5 x 4½
Collection Julius Oppenheimer, New York

*89 EIGHT FIGURES, 1927
Oil on canvas, 18 x 30 inches
Collection Mrs. Nathan J. Miller, New Rochelle, New York

> NOTE: In this study subject matter, attitude and gesture were entirely subsidiary to the problem of form, balance of volume, and sculpturesque spacial values. The seat and back of a long bench within the boundaries of the rectangle make up an arrangement of several horizontal spaces in which the figures are placed. The postures and structure of the figures were ordained more by a plastic necessity than by merely emotional, ideal or decorative interest.—M. W.

90 BALCONY, 1927
Oil on canvas, 18 x 22 inches
Collection Albert Rothbart, New York

91 ZINNIAS, 1927
Oil on canvas, 28 x 20½ inches
Collection The Newark Museum

92 PEWTER CUP, 1928
Lithograph, 8⅜ x 9¾ inches

93 SCULPTOR'S MODEL, 1928
Lithograph, 7⅝ x 4½ inches

*94 STILL LIFE, DISTRIBUTED, 1929
Oil on canvas, 27½ x 35½ inches

> NOTE: An arrangement of simple, familiar objects that would very readily lend itself to an arabesque or decorative treatment, but instead the three dimensional treatment of modelling and color construction was chosen.—M. W.

95 SAND HILLS, 1929
Oil on canvas, 30 x 36 inches

96 STUDY FOR "MUSIC," 1929
Oil on canvas-board, 11¼ x 17¾ inches
Private Collection, New York

*97 HEAD OF A WOMAN, 1929
Drawing on canvas-board, 16 x 13½ inches
Private Collection, New York

*98 TRANQUILITY, 1930
Oil on canvas, 31½ x 40 inches

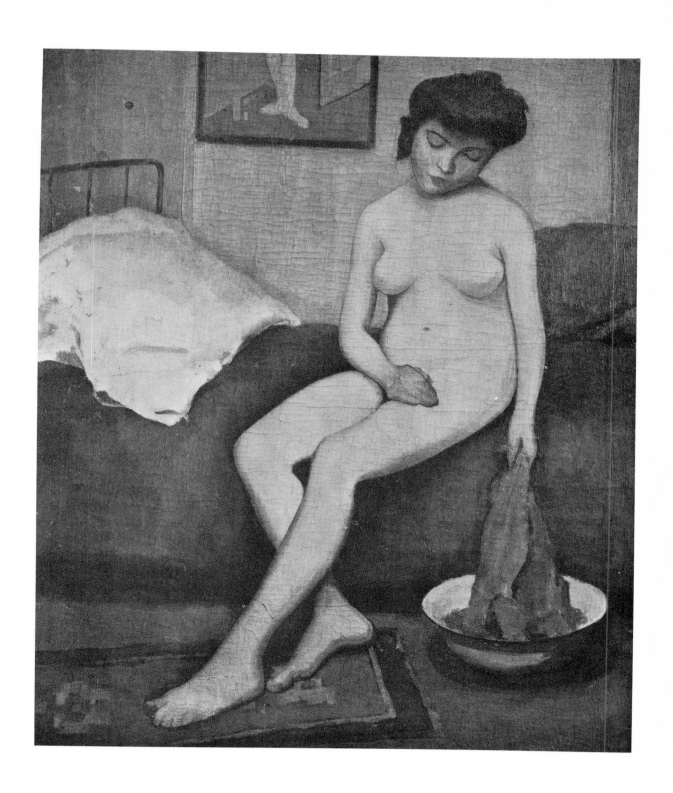

2

THE YOUNG MODEL, 1907
Oil, 38½ x 31½ inches
Collection of the Artist

12
COMPOSITION WITH THREE FIGURES, 1910
Oil, 47 x 23 ½ inches
Collection of the Artist

19
THE GERANIUM, 1911
Oil, 39¼ x 31¾ inches
Collection of the Artist

27
DECORATION WITH CLOUD, 1913
Oil, 59¼ x 40 inches
Collection of the Artist

31
MAINE, 1914
Pastel, 24½ x 18 inches
Collection of the Artist

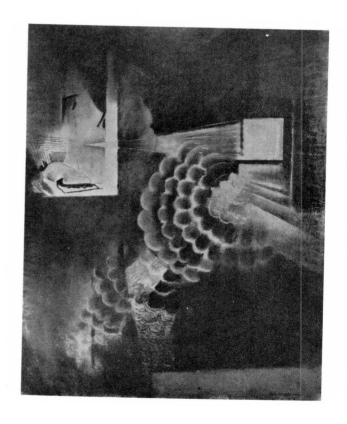

42
LECTURE, METROPOLITAN MUSEUM, 1917
Pastel, 24¼ x 18 inches
Collection of the Artist

35
NEW YORK AT NIGHT, 1915
Oil, 34 x 22 inches
Collection of the Artist

39
THE PIQUÉ SHIRT, 1916
Oil, 31 x 24 inches
Collection of the Artist

45
THE CELLIST, 1917
Oil, 39¾ x 29½ inches
Collection of the Artist

48
THE SISTERS, 1917
Oil, 36 x 17¾ inches
Collection of the Artist

60
THE DRAMATIST, 1918
Gouache, 4½ x 4½ inches
Private Collection, New York

97
HEAD OF A WOMAN, 1929
Charcoal, 16 x 13½ inches
Private Collection, New York

74
INVOCATION, 1919
Oil, 48 x 41 ½ inches
Collection of the Artist

83
THE RIVER, 1926
Oil, 24½ x 29½ inches
Collection of the Artist

87
OLD BARNS, 1926
Oil, 25 x 30 inches
Collection Dr. B. D. Saklatwalla, Crafton, Pennsylvania

89
EIGHT FIGURES, 1927
Oil, 18 x 30 inches
Collection Mrs. Nathan J. Miller, New Rochelle, New York

94
STILL LIFE, DISTRIBUTED, 1929
Oil, 27½ x 35½ inches
Collection of the Artist

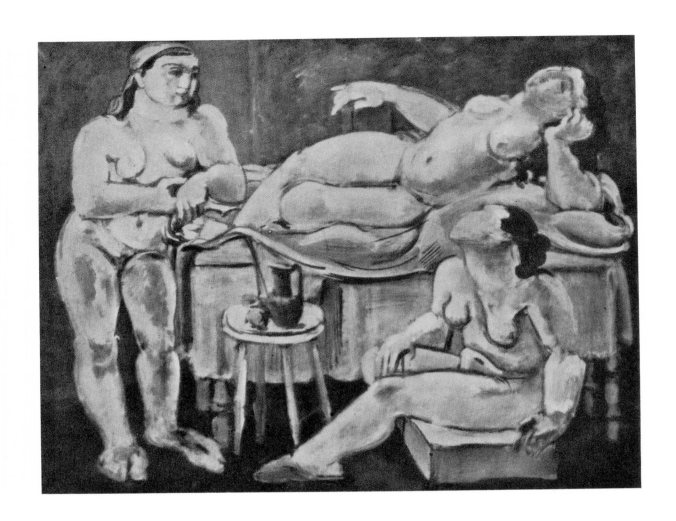

98
TRANQUILITY, 1930
Oil, 31 ½ x 40 inches
Collection of the Artist

This catalog was issued March eleventh nineteen thirty, by the Trustees of The Museum of Modern Art, in New York. One thousand copies.

PLANDOME PRESS, INC., NEW YORK, N. Y.

MAURICE STERNE

MAURICE STERNE

RETROSPECTIVE EXHIBITION 1902-1932

PAINTINGS · SCULPTURE · DRAWINGS

FEBRUARY 15TH   1933   MARCH 25TH

THE MUSEUM OF MODERN ART

11 WEST 53RD STREET · NEW YORK

TRUSTEES

THE EXHIBITION HAS BEEN SELECTED FROM THE FOLLOWING COLLECTIONS:

DR. AND MRS. JOSEPH ASCH, NEW YORK

MR. STEPHAN BOURGEOIS, NEW YORK

DR. A. A. BRILL, NEW YORK

MR. AND MRS. RICHARD BRIXEY, NEW YORK

MR. EDWARD BRUCE, WASHINGTON

MISS MABEL CHOATE, NEW YORK

MRS. W. MURRAY CRANE, NEW YORK

MR. FRANK CROWNINSHIELD, NEW YORK

LORD DUVEEN OF MILLBANK, NEW YORK

HERR ADOLF FISCHER, DÜSSELDORF

HERR ALFRED FLECHTHEIM, BERLIN

MR. AND MRS. BERTRAM FOX, NEW YORK

MRS. JOHN W. GARRETT, ROME

MR. GEORGE GERSHWIN, NEW YORK

MR. LAWRENCE GILMAN, NEW YORK

MR. A. CONGER GOODYEAR, NEW YORK

MR. CARL HAMILTON, PARIS

MRS. MEREDITH HARE, COLORADO SPRINGS

MR. HUNT HENDERSON, NEW ORLEANS

MR. AND MRS. WALTER HOCHSCHILD, NEW YORK

MR. EDWARD J. HOLMES, BOSTON

DR. AND MRS. HORACE KALLEN, NEW YORK

MR. ROBERT LAURENT, BROOKLYN

MR. AND MRS. ARTHUR LEHMAN, NEW YORK

MR. ADOLPH LEWISOHN, NEW YORK

MR. FRANK LEWISOHN, NEW YORK

MR. AND MRS. SAMUEL A. LEWISOHN, NEW YORK

MRS. CHARLES J. LIEBMAN, NEW YORK

MR. HARRY T. LINDEBERG, NEW YORK

MR. AND MRS. WALTER LIPPMANN, NEW YORK

MRS. MABEL DODGE LUHAN, TAOS, NEW MEXICO

MRS. ROBERT T. McKEE, NEW YORK

HERR HEINRICH NAUEN, DÜSSELDORF

MR. HAROLD WOODBURY PARSONS, BOSTON

MME. LILI DU BOIS REYMOND, GERMANY

MRS. JACKSON REYNOLDS, NEW YORK

MRS. CHARLES A. ROBINSON, JR., PROVIDENCE
MRS. JOHN D. ROCKEFELLER, JR., NEW YORK
MRS. PHILIP J. ROOSEVELT, NEW YORK
MR. ALBERT ROTHBART, NEW YORK
MR. PAUL J. SACHS, CAMBRIDGE
MR. WALTER E. SACHS, NEW YORK
MR. HENRY SHEAFER, POTTSVILLE, PENNSYLVANIA
MR. AND MRS. LESLEY GREEN SHEAFER, NEW YORK
MR. AND MRS. GEORGE A. SPIEGELBERG, NEW YORK
MR. MAURICE STERNE, NEW YORK
MRS. MAURICE STERNE, NEW YORK
MRS. ROYALL VICTOR, SYOSSET, NEW YORK
HERR ALEX VÖMEL, DÜSSELDORF
MRS. ALMA WERTHEIM, NEW YORK
MRS. FRANCES M. WOLCOTT, NEW YORK
MUSEUM OF FINE ARTS, BOSTON
THE BROOKLYN MUSEUM
CARNEGIE INSTITUTE, PITTSBURGH
THE ART INSTITUTE OF CHICAGO
THE CLEVELAND MUSEUM OF ART
THE CORCORAN GALLERY OF ART, WASHINGTON
THE DETROIT INSTITUTE OF ARTS
THE METROPOLITAN MUSEUM OF ART, NEW YORK
PHILLIPS MEMORIAL GALLERY, WASHINGTON
RHODE ISLAND SCHOOL OF DESIGN MUSEUM OF ART, PROVIDENCE
FINE ARTS GALLERY, SAN DIEGO
WALLRAF-RICHARTZ MUSEUM, COLOGNE
GALLERY OF FINE ARTS, YALE UNIVERSITY, NEW HAVEN
GALERIE ALFRED FLECHTHEIM, BERLIN AND DÜSSELDORF
THE MILCH GALLERIES, NEW YORK
THE REINHARDT GALLERIES, NEW YORK

MAURICE STERNE AND HIS TIMES

CONTEMPORARY arts, especially the graphic and plastic arts, are distinguished from those of other ages by the number, the variety and the disputes of sects and schools. The painter or sculptor is rare who achieves distinction on the intrinsic qualities of his work and not because he exemplifies some aesthetic philosophy or some psychological theory of perception and technological theory of execution. The very names of the schools signalize their extra-pictorial preoccupations: "Impressionism," "Post-Impressionism," "Cubism," "Futurism," "Orphism," "Vorticism," "Synchromism," "Dada," "Expressionism." To appreciate and to understand the work of the adherents of these schools, it is necessary to know their sources and backgrounds as well as to perceive their content. For many schools define themselves even more by that which they oppose and deny than by that which they propose and affirm. Their members are really metaphysicians and psychologists. Their creations speak by preference to the *cognoscenti;* they make no communication to the masses of men.

Now, all works of art arise in one plane of life and survive or perish in another. In their origins, they are personal to the artist. They are events in his biography and project and express all the varied forces which act upon his passions and imagination—his hopes and fears and loves and hates, his perceptions and judgments and valuations. Truly to understand the origin and personal significance of the artist's works it would be necessary to realize the world of men and things in which he lives, what he fears, what he hates, whom he envies, whom he despises, what he desires and what disgusts him. All such objects, as they enter or leave the artist's experience, modify and transform his personality. They alter its stances and transitions, change its tempo, and finally come together in his imagination as a characteristic, recurrent visual pattern, with its unique organization, progression and rhythm.

So with the art of Maurice Sterne. It is shaped by a relentless inward *élan* which carries him through life undisturbed by the clamors of the market and the views and disputes of the schools. Sterne's craftsmanship, his sense of the technical problems of material and medium, his iconography and vision grow out of the work itself. Easily at home amid all the changes and chances of the world of modern art since its beginnings at the turn of the century, he seems nevertheless to have gone his own way undistracted by it, assimilating into his own vision its relevancies, and shedding its irrelevancies as a duck sheds water. Looking at his

7

work as a whole, we see it presenting the paradox of extraordinary contemporaneity all suffused with an equally extraordinary traditionality. Completely of our own time, it is still our own day's embodiment and projection of the living past, so do serenity and force interpenetrate in it, so builded is it of moving rhythms in a balanced round. It exemplifies no school; it calls for no special psychology or aesthetic theory; and it speaks with the same clarity and appeal to the masses as to the experts.

The emergence of Sterne's characteristic iconography and pictorial vision is a slow and not steady process. The pictures he painted between 1897 and 1904 show the beginner's natural concern with the quality of paint, tonal values and linear grace. His line is rhythmic but lacks force. The compositions completed between 1904 and 1907 show a growing endeavor after force. The grace is as much as ever present, but one observes stress on volume, on the organization of masses in harmonious and dynamic patterns. Between 1907 and 1911—Sterne was in Europe—the characteristic Sterne signature becomes manifest. One senses enormous labor, constant elimination, selection, simplification. Finally one encounters that compelling and powerful line which encloses form but is no frame for it, which generates contour and structure in a single, continuous movement, that sets before us simultaneously both the mass of the figure and the pull which gravity exercises on it. The later paintings—whether executed in Italy or Bali or the United States—the sculptures and the drawings, more and more emerge as vigor and grace of meaning achieved through the simplest and most economical of means. The paintings exemplify a growing interest in chiaroscuro, in that visual ambiguity of spatial orders (which the *Gestalt* school of psychologists regard as so significant), in the means of stating three-dimensional relationships of movement and repose in the two-dimensional medium of the painter. Like Whistler, with whom in his youth he was sometimes compared, Sterne occasionally speaks of painting in the language of music. He has a sense of space as a symbol for time, and seeks, with a strict regard for the integrity of his medium, to perfect "a pictorial art resembling music and literature;" to produce in painting by means of unmistakable symbols, clear and distinct, a sort of instant music compounded of spatial orders. This is his present aim. This is the goal which the pictures produced since 1930 drive at.

The biographical background out of which these phases lift themselves as the high professional points, seems all inward detachment amid much outward tur-

8

moil and adventure. Maurice Sterne was born in 1878 in the Baltic city of Libau, when that was a part of the dominion of the Russian Tsar. He was the youngest in a family of five brothers and sisters, all talented, some devoted to music, some to science, and all to the revolutionary idealism characteristic of the Russian intellectuals of the period. As a child, he attended the Technical School of Moscow, and was thus early set in a milieu where precise form was of paramount importance. Family exigencies moved him from Libau to Moscow, and from Moscow to New York. In New York, he and his family were confronted with the bitter problems of a living and a life so common among high-minded and impoverished immigrants. Some time after his arrival, at the age of twelve, Sterne was apprenticed to an engraver. His new occupation was concerned with the engraving of maps by means of a wax process. The wax invited manipulation and modelling, on its own account, and Sterne did not resist the invitation. He would in free interludes shape wax figures on the copper plate.

Advised that his chances of advancement in the craft would be greatly improved if he learned mechanical drawing, he joined the evening classes at Cooper Union, but found himself without interest in mechanical drawing. Instead of doing his stint, he made sketches of his fellow students and drew figures. One day his teacher discovered him at it, and suggested his joining the life class in the National Academy. He followed the suggestion gladly and was fascinated by the casts which he was first set to draw. His interest in engraving grew laxer than ever. Finally his employer told him that he was a disappointment and discharged him.

Sterne was both relieved and disturbed. He wanted to spend his whole day in drawing and painting, but he had to make a living. Through a friend he found a job working at night. All day he studied at the National Academy. At night he worked at his job, snatching what sleep he could. After four years of study at the Academy, he decided to compete for all the prizes which it offered. He won every competition and was enabled to give up his night job. He was appointed assistant to James D. Smillie and thus began his long teaching career. His labors as a teacher have played an important part in the realization and mastery of his own problems.

As one follows his performance from the examples first shown, thirty years ago, in the Old Country Sketch Club on Broadway, to the paintings never before exhibited, one sees the register of the world of art through which Sterne moved but on which his vision would not let him dwell. In the early pictures

9

there are suggestions of Manet and Whistler. Indeed some of Sterne's work was mistaken, and bought, for Whistler's, although Sterne had never seen an actual Whistler in his life. Max J. Friedlander, the director of the Kupferstitch Kabinet in Berlin, referred to Sterne as only second to Whistler among all Americans who had exercised a world-wide influence on graphic art. A little later, when Sterne was sojourning in Europe as the first traveling fellow ever appointed by the National Academy of Design, he came into contact with the protagonists of the new movement in Paris, but his dominant interest was in the works of the masters in the museums. Mantegna and Pollaiuolo came closer to providing what his heart was seeking. He left France for Italy, and from Italy he went to Greece. Sculpture allured him. He labored to state volume and mass by means of the dynamic line, so that the tri-dimensional weight and thrust of sculpture shall be communicated by the two-dimensional swing of line and shape. Sculptural form obsessed him. When he returned to Italy he started modelling in wax, on a plaster base. The outcome of his effort was the famous *Pasquale* or Bomb-Thrower which is in the Metropolitan Museum in New York. He took to wax spontaneously, without reflection. It was the medium of his boyhood in the engraver's shop. Meanwhile paintings of his were shown in the Paris Salon where they received favorable mention.

A series of accidents took Sterne to India, from India to Java, from Java to Bali. In Bali he settled down for a period of two years. For various reasons it was a dark time in his life, and its darkness was projected in many of the drawings and paintings of the period. During his three years' stay, more or less, in Bali, he produced several thousand studies and drawings in various degrees of completion. The sheer quantity is sufficient indication of the masterful technique, of the practically infallible control of the medium. Sterne appears easily as the paramount draftsman of our time. Whatever the Bali picture, however sombre its tone, it impresses with the unfailing firmness and drive of the austere, unbroken line of composition. Occasionally one comes upon comparisons of Sterne's Bali pictures with Gauguin's South Sea paintings. But merely to put a Sterne and a Gauguin side by side is to recognize how distinct, independent, and remote from each other are the two idioms.

By 1914 Sterne seems to have found himself. He returned to the United States. His stay in America is one series of experiments after another with paint and other media. In Croton-on-Hudson, in Maine on Monhegan Island, in New Mexico, he experimented with this new medium and that. Wax continued to

10

interest him. He tried it as a medium for oil paints in rock and other studies; for fixing chalk and charcoal. As themes he found the Indians of New Mexico deeply attractive. There was a resurgence of his sculptural interest. Again he modeled in wax, those still and forceful Indian heads and the portrait of Senta, which are so like and so unlike the Greek portraits of the classic period.

Sterne's endeavor to state the volume and weight of objects by means of the dynamic line had now developed into a controlled technique wherein the line serves, not merely as a frame enclosing a shape but as a dynamic process of grow-ing out into a contour. In black and white, the quality is that which is some-times found in the *notan* of the Chinese, but *notan* is invariably flat and states the *élan* of living form in linear dimension only. In Sterne's work the line fuses with the color and projects the third dimension. The pictures convey something of the mass and weight which sculpture conveys. Sterne's still lifes and floral pieces make this quality particularly conspicuous. In the flower pieces the struc-tural volume often produces an effect of modernist distortion, and it is in these that Sterne appears as most contemporaneous. The same quality of workman-ship applied to the human figure, gives rise to the impression that the figure is "all there." It is in this that his work is most definitely a prolongation of the great tradition of painting in the western world.

In 1921 Sterne returned to Italy, to the little hamlet of Anticoli in the Sabine hills, that had, largely because of him, become a center for artists of all nation-alities, American included. There he painted the compositions in which his style reaches its maturity. There he modeled that figure of self-contained harmony known as *The Awakening*. There he thought out and executed the noble monument of *The Pilgrim Pioneers*, which stands in Elm Park in Worcester, Massachusetts. In Anticoli, withdrawn from the world of business and the world of art, Sterne clarified and defined his vision of both these worlds and his philosophy of life. This philosophy, expressed in his art, seeks serenity without illusion, inwardness without distortion. Both his painting and his sculpture communicate, in an iconography entirely contemporary, the calm which is above the battle though its symbols are the figures and the relationships of the battle itself. Therein is again embodied the kinship of Sterne's work with the tradition of the masters in the pictorial arts. It carries out to the exigencies of the present hour the enduring meanings of the living past.

In this projection, each specific ethos of time and place interfuses with the others like the tones of a melody, and, cleared of its local reference and temporary signification, becomes a generalized expression of the perennial passions of the human heart. Consider the painting known as *Sacrifice,* in the Adolph Lewisohn collection. The composition of this picture is characteristic. By many it is regarded as perhaps the greatest of Sterne's paintings. Try to find out why, and you are struck with the realization that its theme renews, with a contemporary pertinency, a great traditional focus of emotion of the western world. The massive traditional emotion is aroused without our knowing it and drained as it is aroused, utterly and completely, by the dominant patterns of the design and the order of the painting *qua* painting. The picture exercises on the beholder an unfailing fascination of pity and delight.

This is the quality of Sterne's work at its height. It is conspicuous in his sculpture and recurrent in his paintings. Its serenity, living, without softness, brings complete relief from the excitement, the turgidity, and the strain, which characterize so much that is usually called modern in the pictorial arts. Signs are not lacking that the generation now growing up has done with this passing turbulence. The recognition which has come to Sterne in recent years is one of the signs that the stream of living art has flowed beyond its rapids into the deeper, stronger and stiller channels of the imaginative life.

H. M. Kallen

A NOTE BY THE ARTIST

IN making the selection for my present retrospective exhibition we were guided by two principles. We wished to show the most characteristic examples of each period and to present a rhythmic and unbroken sequence in order that the whole should become consequential and correlated. When we had made up the list we discovered that we had selected more than twice as many works as could be placed advantageously. This made it necessary to leave out many examples which would have provided the necessary shading between one period and its immediate background and foreground. It was then decided to show only the most characteristic and successful examples of each period. It is just as well, for even if the opportunity should arise to present a man's work in its entirety, it would be impossible to do so. The records showing years of experimentation and searching, which are the destiny of every serious painter of our time, have often been destroyed by the artist. These cannot be resurrected.

It was different when a living vital tradition was handed down by master to disciple. Then the road was clear and open. It was not necessary to blast one's path through a jungle. Art was not an adventure, as it is to-day, but a well-planned journey. In art expression three main agencies function: impulse, environment, and tradition. When any of these is lacking the result is bound to be incomplete.

Among my memorable experiences during a lengthy sojourn in British India, Burma, Java and Bali, I often recall frequent visits to the shops where images were produced for the temples. These images were mostly trite and superficial. In the present environment the incentive for art expression is lacking, but those works, nevertheless, show extraordinary precision and craftsmanship. The planning, method and execution are traditional. The sculptor I watched in Java had undoubtedly inherited his technique from the same sources which created the sublime carvings at the Temple of Boro-Budur. I became convinced that in the East a true art tradition is still alive but for some reason the true instinct is lacking. It is as if one inherited a beautiful language without having anything to say. In the West, on the other hand, there are many who have something significant to communicate but not the adequate means of expression.

Unless we have the good fortune to discover a Virgil to show us the way, we are bound to land in the *Inferno* and stay there. The question—Where are the Virgils?—is easy to answer. They are in the museums. But which of them to

13

select as guides? That is a difficult problem which each artist must settle for himself. In our time we must be guided wholly by our instinct—conquer the limitations of time and space and receive a direct message from the significant works of the past. The revelations of the past should not only be our guide but a test of our accomplishment. The stimulus must come from our environment. After all, the immortal *Divina Commedia* was created by Dante—not by Virgil.

When the works for the present exhibition had been assembled I realized that the three essentials which have guided me and which I endeavored to fuse in one are instinct, environment, and tradition. The road is a difficult one. But I feel that I have emerged from the *selva oscura* and if I should have the good fortune to live twenty-five years longer I hope to come much nearer to my goal.

MAURICE STERNE

CHRONOLOGY

1878   Born at Libau on the Baltic.

1889   To New York with widowed mother.

1891   Designer's helper in a map engraving house.

1892   Studied mechanical drawing at Cooper Union. His professor, a Mr. Strong, taught him free-hand drawing when he discovered that Sterne, like Whistler, "covered his mechanical efforts with others done in freehand."

1894–99   Attended National Academy of Design. Studied anatomy with Thomas Eakins, who came from Philadelphia once a week to teach.

1900–1902   Made series of etchings, including Coney Island set.

1902   First exhibition of paintings at Old Country Sketch Club, New York. William M. Chase purchased one of his canvases.

1903   Assisted James D. Smillie as instructor of etching.

1904   Won Mooney Travelling Scholarship at National Academy of Design, for composition.

1904–1908   To Europe. Visited studios in Paris, but mostly studied masters in museums. Traveled in France, Germany, Italy. Studied especially the work of Mantegna, Pollaiuolo, and Piero della Francesca, and among the moderns Manet, and Cézanne.

1908   To Greece. Studied Greek art in Athens, especially in the Parthenon Museum. Spent six weeks at Delphi studying the Delphic charioteer of which he made many studies. Began his first sculpture. Lived eight months in a monastery at Mt. Hymettos.

1910   Exhibition of drawings and etchings at gallery of Paul Cassierer, Berlin. Etchings acquired by Kaiser Friederich Museum, Berlin.

1911   To Egypt. Studied Egyptian art, mostly in upper Egypt. Then to British India where he spent eight months, four of them at Benares studying the panorama of its religious life from a boat on the Ganges.

1912   To Burma where he spent four months, mostly in Mandalay. Made many studies and drawings in the Golden Pagoda.

1912 Cont'd	To Java for two months. Then to Bali where he spent two years. Made several thousand drawings and paintings (many of them in oil on thin rice paper) of Balinese life.
	Exhibition of paintings and drawings done in Italy up to the year 1910, at the Berlin Photographic Company, New York, in January.
1914	Returned to Italy in August, and then to New York, where he arrived in January, 1915.
1915	Exhibition of work done in Bali at the Berlin Photographic Company, New York.
1915–16	Lived at Croton-on-Hudson, New York, painting.
1917	To New Mexico where he spent a year, mostly in Taos. One-man show at the Art Institute of Chicago, in January.
	Exhibition of series of rock studies of the Maine coast, flower pieces, and drawings in ink and crayon, at the Bourgeois Galleries, New York, in March and April.
1918	Returned to Anticoli-Corrado, Italy, where he had already spent several years before the war.
1919	Returned to America. Exhibited at the Boston Art Club in February.
1922	Exhibition of paintings, drawings and sculptures at the Bourgeois Galleries in April.
1925	Invited to represent America at the Third Biennial International Exhibition in Rome, where three galleries were devoted to his work—paintings, drawings, and one sculpture, *The Awakening*. Invited to paint self-portrait for the Uffizi Gallery in Florence.
1926	Awarded commission for Rogers-Kennedy Memorial, Worcester, Massachusetts.
	Exhibited at Scott & Fowles, New York.
1928	Exhibited at the Reinhardt Galleries, New York, in February.
	Exhibited at the Art Institute of Chicago where he won Logan medal and prize of $750.
1929	*Monument to Early Settlers* (Rogers-Kennedy Memorial) unveiled on December 6th at Elm Park, Worcester, Massachusetts.
	Elected president of Society of American Painters, Sculptors and Gravers.

1930   Awarded first William A. Clark prize of $2,000 and Corcoran gold medal for *After Lunch* at the 12th Annual Exhibition of Contemporary American Oil Painting, Corcoran Gallery of Art, Washington, D. C.

Honorable mention for *High School Girl* at 29th Carnegie Institute International Exhibition at Pittsburgh, Pa.

Exhibition of drawings at the Reinhardt Galleries, New York, in May.

1932   Living at Anticoli-Corrado, painting.

Exhibited in the International Art Exhibition in Venice, Italy; in "American Painting and Sculpture, 1862–1932," exhibition at Museum of Modern Art, New York; and in First Biennial Exhibition of Contemporary American Painting, Whitney Museum of American Art, New York.

1933   Exhibited in College Art Association's "International 1933" shown at Worcester (Massachusetts) Art Museum in January and at Rockefeller Center, New York, in February.

MAURICE STERNE

BIBLIOGRAPHY

ANONYMOUS, *The Monumental Simplicity in the Pictorial Art of Maurice Sterne.* Current Opinion, LIX, Dec. 1915, pp. 425–27

BIRNBAUM, MARTIN, *Introductions; painters, sculptors, and graphic artists.* New York, Frederick Fairchild Sherman, 1919, pp. 40–50

————, *Maurice Sterne.* International Studio, XLVI, Mar. 1912, supplement pp. III–XIII

BOSTON, MUSEUM OF FINE ARTS, *"The Awakening," by Maurice Sterne.* Bulletin, XXV, June 1927, pp. 35–36

DEFRIES, A. D., *Maurice Sterne at Bali.* International Studio, LXI, Apr. 1917, supplement LIII–LVI

DUBOIS, G. P., *Chance and an Art Career.* New York Herald Tribune, July 13, 1930, magazine section, pp. 14–15 and 22

FREUND, F. E. W., *Amerikanische Künstlerprofile; 1. Maurice Sterne. Jahrbuch der Jungen Kunst.* Leipzig, Klinkhardt & Biermann, 1921, pp. 305–09

GIBSON, LILLIAN, *Perpetuating a New World Epic.* American Hebrew, CXXVII, May 23, 1930, pp. 17 and 71

KOOTZ, S. M., *Modern American Painters.* New York, Brewer & Warren, Inc., 1930, pp. 53–54

McBRIDE, HENRY, *News and Comment in the World of Art.* New York Sun, Jan. 14, 1917, section 5, p. 12

MORGAN, A. deG., *Maurice Sterne.* Junior League Magazine, XVI, Jan. 1930, pp. 49–50

PHILLIPS, DUNCAN, *A Collection in the Making.* Washington, Phillips Memorial Gallery, 1926, p. 61, plates CIII, CIV, CV, CVI, CVII

————, *Derain and the New Dignity in Painting.* Art and Understanding, Washington, Phillips Memorial Gallery, Vol. 1, Nov. 1929, pp. 87–89

————, *The Artist Sees Differently.* Washington, Phillips Memorial Gallery, 1931, vol. 1, pp. 17, 52, 71, 96–97, and 99

STEIN, LEO, *Tradition and Art*. The Arts, VII, May 1925, pp. 265–69

STERNE, MAURICE, *Introduction to catalogue of exhibition of drawings and paintings by Maurice Sterne at the Berlin Photographic Co.*, New York, 1915

————, *Introduction to catalogue of exhibition of paintings, drawings and sculpture by Maurice Sterne*, Bourgeois Gallery, Apr. 1922

————, *Conservative Youth*. Taken from report of an interview with Maurice Sterne by Louis Sherwin of the New York Post. Art Digest, VI, Jan. 15, 1932, p. 29

————, *Nationalism in Art—Is It an Advantage?* Report of a debate at the Whitney Museum of American Art, in which Maurice Sterne argued for the negative. Art Digest, VI, Apr. 1, 1932, pp. 15–16, 21

————, *New Society Reorganized under Old Name*. Art News, XXVIII, Apr. 19, 1930, p. 8

TATLOCK, R. R., *Tatlock Praises Worcester Memorial by Maurice Sterne*. Art News, XXVIII, Feb. 1, 1930, pp. 22–23

TAVOLATO, ITALO, *Maurice Sterne*. Rome, Valori Plastici, 1925.

YOUNG, STARK, *A New Monument*. New Republic, LXI, Dec. 25, 1929, pp. 142–43

————, *Maurice Sterne's Exhibition*. New Republic, XLV, Feb. 17, 1926, p. 355

————, *The Mould of Form*. A Drawing by Maurice Sterne. New Republic, XXXIII, Jan. 3, 1923, p. 149

CATALOG

OILS

An asterisk before a catalog number indicates that the
work is illustrated by a plate bearing the same number.

1 BEATRICE, 1902
   Oil on canvas, 54 x 38 inches
   Collection Mrs. Royall Victor, Syosset, New York

2 CLARA, 1903
   Oil on canvas, 73 x 36 inches
   Collection the Artist

3 JULIETTE, 1905
   Oil on canvas, 25 1/4 x 20 1/8 inches
   Collection Henry Sheafer, Pottsville, Pennsylvania

4 GIRL'S PROFILE, 1905
   Oil on canvas, 24 x 18 inches
   Collection The Milch Galleries, New York

5 CAIN AND ABEL, 1907
   Oil on canvas, 29 x 33 inches
   Collection Robert Laurent, Brooklyn

6 BENARES, 1911
   Oil on canvas, 39 x 30 1/2 inches
   Collection The Milch Galleries, New York

7 PRAYING PILGRIM, BENARES, 1911
   Oil on paper, 23 x 15 inches
   Collection The Milch Galleries, New York

8 GREETING THE SUN, BENARES, 1912
   Oil on canvas, 32 x 38 inches
   Private Collection

9 RESTING AT THE BAZAAR, 1912
   Oil on canvas, 26 3/4 x 31 1/2 inches
   Private Collection

10 BALI DRAMA, 1912
   Oil on canvas, 24⅝ x 26½ inches
   Collection Fine Arts Gallery, San Diego

   (Removed by the Society's special permission from a circuit sponsored by the Western Association of Art Museum Directors.)

11 DANCE OF DEATH, 1912
   Oil on canvas, 35½ x 32 inches
   Collection the Artist

12 BENARES GHATS, 1912
   Oil on canvas, 17½ x 23 inches
   Collection The Milch Galleries, New York

13 BALI WOMAN CARRYING BASKET, 1912
   Oil on paper
   Private Collection

14 BALI, 1912
   Oil on paper, 24⅛ x 15 inches
   Collection Miss Mabel Choate, New York

15 BENARES, 1912
   Oil on paper, 19¼ x 20⅝ inches
   Collection Miss Mabel Choate, New York

16 MANDALAY, 1912
   Oil on paper, 17 x 18 inches
   Collection Miss Mabel Choate, New York

17 ON THE ISLE OF BALI, 1912
   Oil on paper, 21 x 12½ inches
   Collection The Art Institute of Chicago

18 LEANING FIGURE, BALI
   Oil on paper, 18 x 9 inches
   Collection Robert Laurent, Brooklyn

19 BAZAAR, BALI, 1913
   Oil on canvas, 38¼ x 28¾ inches
   Private Collection

24

*20 DANCE OF THE ELEMENTS, BALI, 1913
   Oil on canvas, 57 x 65 inches
   Private Collection

21 TEMPLE DANCERS, BALI, 1913
   Oil on canvas, 34 x 30 inches
   Private Collection

22 NIGHT TEMPLE FEAST, BALI, 1913
   Oil on canvas, 39 x 36 inches
   Collection the Artist

23 WOMAN AND CHILD, BALI, 1913
   Oil on paper, 13¾ x 15½ inches
   Collection George Gershwin, New York

24 TWO GIRLS SEATED ON A WALL, 1913
   Oil on paper, 12½ x 16 inches
   Collection Mrs. Meredith Hare, Colorado Springs

25 BALI, 1913
   Oil on paper, 10½ x 7¾ inches
   Collection Alfred Flechtheim, Berlin

26 BALI WOMAN, 1913
   Oil on paper, 17½ x 10½ inches
   Collection Albert Rothbart, New York

27 BALI CARNIVAL, 1913
   Oil on paper, 20 x 16 inches
   Collection the Artist

28 BALI GIRL, 1913
   Oil on paper, 11 x 7½ inches
   Collection the Artist

29 BALI MASK, 1913
   Oil on paper, 17½ x 16 inches
   Collection the Artist

30 BALI WOMAN STANDING, 1913
   Oil on paper, 20 x 10¾ inches
   Collection the Artist

31 BALI WOMAN WITH LITTLE PIG, 1913
Oil on paper, 21 x 8¾ inches
Collection the Artist

32 MOTHER AND CHILD AT BAZAAR, 1914
Oil on canvas
Collection Walter E. Sachs, New York

33 BAZAAR, BALI, 1914
Oil on canvas, 36 x 39 inches
Collection The Milch Galleries, New York

*34 TEMPLE FEAST, BALI, 1914
Oil on canvas, 39 x 42½ inches
Collection The Milch Galleries, New York

35 CREMATION, BALI, 1914
Oil on canvas, 25½ x 30½ inches
Collection Reinhardt Galleries, New York

36 FIGURE OF WOMAN, BALI, 1914
Oil on paper
Collection Harold Woodbury Parsons, Boston

37 BAZAAR SKETCH, 1914
Oil on paper
Private Collection, New York

38 BALI WOMAN, 1914
Oil on paper, 20 x 14½ inches
Collection Lili Du Bois Reymond, Germany

39 GROUP OF WOMEN, BALI, 1914
Oil on paper, 16½ x 19 inches
Collection Mrs. Vera Sterne, New York

40 MOTHER AND CHILD, 1914
Oil on paper, 22 x 14 inches
Collection Rhode Island School of Design Museum of Art, Providence

41 BAZAAR, BALI, 1914
Oil on paper, 22 x 17 inches
Collection The Milch Galleries, New York

42 BALI GIRL, 1914
Oil on paper, 21 x 11 inches
Collection Reinhardt Galleries, New York

43 LILIES, 1915
Oil on paper
Collection Mr. and Mrs. Walter Lippmann, New York

44 GREEN BOWL, TULIPS, 1916
Oil on canvas, 21¾ x 24½ inches
Collection Mrs. Meredith Hare, Colorado Springs

45 POTTSVILLE, PENNSYLVANIA, 1916
Oil on canvas, 28 x 32¼ inches
Collection the Artist

46 TULIPS, 1917
Oil on canvas, 25 x 25 inches
Collection Lawrence Gilman, New York

47 ANGELINA ASLEEP, 1918
Oil on canvas, 20 x 24¾ inches
Private Collection

48 FLOWERS, 1918
Oil on canvas, 33 x 22 inches
Collection Frank Lewisohn, New York

49 INDIAN HEAD, 1918
Oil on Chinese paper, 16¾ x 12¼ inches
Collection Hunt Henderson, New Orleans

*50 SACRIFICE, 1919
Oil on canvas, 46 x 39¼ inches
Collection Adolph Lewisohn, New York

51 ANTICOLI LANDSCAPE, 1920
Oil on canvas, 27 x 25 inches
Gladys Roosevelt Dick Collection, New York

52 POPPIES, 1920
Oil on canvas
Private Collection, New York

53 MARCELLA, 1920
   Oil on canvas, 19 x 15 inches
   Private Collection

54 THE WINDING PATH, 1922
   Oil on canvas, 45¾ x 34 inches
   Collection Adolph Lewisohn, New York

55 THE OFFERING, 1922
   Oil on canvas, 44 x 27 inches
   Private Collection

56 WOMAN'S HEAD, 1922
   Oil on panel, 15½ x 12½ inches
   Collection The Milch Galleries, New York

*57 BREAD MAKERS, 1923
   Oil on canvas, 49 x 33¼ inches
   Private Collection

*58 EGGS WITH CARAFE, 1923
   Oil on canvas, 16½ x 19 inches
   Collection Mr. and Mrs. Samuel A. Lewisohn, New York

*59 INEZ, 1923
   Oil on canvas, 52½ x 40¾ inches
   Collection Lord Duveen of Millbank, New York

60 GREEN APPLES, 1924
   Oil on canvas, 27½ x 34⅝ inches
   Collection Edward J. Holmes, Boston

61 MOTHER AND CHILD, 1924
   Oil on canvas, 26 x 17¾ inches
   Collection Edward Bruce, Washington

62 NASTURTIUMS, 1924
   Oil on canvas, 18½ x 14⅛ inches
   Collection Edward J. Holmes, Boston

63 STILL LIFE, FIGS, 1924
   Oil on canvas
   Private Collection, New York

*64 AFTERNOON, 1924
   Oil on canvas, 45 x 32 inches
   Collection Phillips Memorial Gallery, Washington

65 BALINESE HEAD, 1924
   Oil on paper
   Collection Mrs. Alma Wertheim, New York

66 GIOVANINA, 1925
   Oil on canvas, 33¾ x 27¾ inches
   Private Collection

67 KEKKINA, 1925
   Oil on canvas
   Collection Mrs. John W. Garrett, Rome

68 LUISETTE, 1925
   Oil on canvas, 22 x 16 inches
   Collection Mrs. Jackson Reynolds, New York

69 REAPERS, 1925
   Oil on canvas, 27¾ x 49 inches
   Collection Phillips Memorial Gallery, Washington

70 STILL LIFE, 1925
   Oil on canvas, 20 x 24¾ inches
   Collection Phillips Memorial Gallery, Washington

71 BLUE VASE AND FLOWERS, 1926
   Oil on canvas, 30¾ x 36½ inches
   Collection Mrs. Robert T. McKee, New York

72 BOWL OF APPLES, 1926
   Oil on canvas, 22½ x 26 inches
   Collection Mr. and Mrs. Lesley Green Sheafer, New York

73 ORANGE AND YELLOW FLOWERS, 1927
   Oil on canvas, 19 x 25 inches
   Private Collection, New York

74 BOWL OF FRUIT, 1928
   Oil on canvas, 18¾ x 24¾ inches
   Collection The Cleveland Museum of Art, Hinman B. Hurlbut Collection

75 BETTINA, 1928
Oil on canvas, 18¼ x 14⅜ inches
Collection Mr. and Mrs. Samuel A. Lewisohn, New York

76 FLOWERS, 1928
Oil on canvas, 29 x 24 inches
Collection Mrs. Charles J. Liebman, New York

77 FLOWERS, 1928
Oil on canvas
Private Collection, New York

*78 GIRL IN BLUE CHAIR, 1928
Oil on canvas, 34 x 24 inches
Collection Mr. and Mrs. Samuel A. Lewisohn, New York

79 GIRL WITH BLACKBERRIES, 1928
Oil on canvas, 37½ x 45 inches
Collection The Detroit Institute of Arts

80 PEARS, 1928
Oil on canvas, 22 x 17 inches
Collection Reinhardt Galleries, New York

*81 THE OLD MILL, 1928
Oil on panel, 50 x 40½ inches
Collection Reinhardt Galleries, New York

82 BLUE DISH, 1929
Oil on canvas, 18 x 22 inches
Collection Mr. and Mrs. Arthur Lehman, New York

83 HIGH SCHOOL GIRL, 1929
Oil on canvas, 50 x 40 inches
Collection Reinhardt Galleries, New York

84 NUDE, 1929
Oil on paper
Collection Adolph Lewisohn, New York

85 TULIPS, 1930
Oil on canvas, 34½ x 24½ inches
Private Collection, New York

86 AFTER LUNCH, 1930
   Oil on panel, 29 x 39 inches
   Collection The Corcoran Gallery of Art, Washington

87 BALI CHILDREN, 1930
   Oil on paper, 18½ x 12¾ inches
   Private Collection, New York

88 BALI GROUP, 1930
   Oil on paper, 16 x 16½ inches
   Collection Reinhardt Galleries, New York

89 STILL LIFE, FRUIT AND EGGS, 1932
   Oil on canvas, 23½ x 29¼ inches
   Collection Mr. and Mrs. Samuel A. Lewisohn, New York

90 GIRL FROM ITALIAN QUARTER, 1932
   Oil on panel, 48½ x 29 inches
   Collection the Artist

91 PEPERONI, 1932
   Oil on panel, 38 x 42½ inches
   Collection Reinhardt Galleries, New York

92 THE AUCTION, 1932
   Oil on panel, 48 x 60 inches
   Collection Reinhardt Galleries, New York

*93 AMERICAN IN ANTICOLI, 1932
   Oil on canvas, 71 x 59 inches
   Collection the Artist

*94 THEME AND VARIATIONS, 1932
   Oil on canvas, 50½ x 39½ inches
   Collection the Artist

95 MARGARET, 1932
   Oil on canvas, 29 x 24 inches
   Collection the Artist

96 GLADYS, 1932
   Oil on canvas, 41 x 30 inches
   Collection the Artist

*97 ASSUNTA, 1932
     Oil on panel, 25½ x 19½ inches
     Collection the Artist

98 HEAD OF CHILD, 1932
     Oil on panel, 15½ x 13½ inches
     Collection the Artist

99 ANTICOLI PERFORMANCE, 1932
     Oil on canvas, 41½ x 40½ inches
     Collection the Artist

100 THE PLUM GIRL, 1932
      Oil on canvas, 52 x 38 inches
      Collection Reinhardt Galleries, New York

101 PEACHES, 1932
      Oil on canvas, 24 x 29 inches
      Collection Reinhardt Galleries, New York

102 STUDY IN PINK AND GREEN, 1932
      Oil on canvas, 25½ x 19½ inches
      Collection the Artist

103 GIRL AT OPEN DOOR, 1932
      Oil on panel, 37½ x 24 inches
      Collection the Artist

DRAWINGS

104 CHILD DRINKING, 1906
      Pen drawing, 12 x 9 inches
      Collection Reinhardt Galleries, New York

*105 ITALIAN BEGGAR, 1906
       Drawing, 16¾ x 14¾ inches
       Collection Mrs. Charles A. Robinson, Jr., Providence

105 HEAD OF AN ITALIAN WOMAN, 1907
      Wash drawing
      Collection Mr. and Mrs. Bertram Fox, New York

107 MAN WITH CLUB (STUDY FOR CAIN AND ABEL), 1907
   Pencil drawing
   Private Collection

108 SEATED NUDE BOY, NO. 1, 1909
   Ink drawing
   Private Collection

109 SEATED NUDE BOY, NO. 2, 1909
   Ink drawing
   Private Collection

110 PORTRAIT OF MY MOTHER, 1909
   Drawing, 17 x 13½ inches
   Collection Museum of Fine Arts, Boston

111 MALE NUDE—THREE-QUARTERS BACK VIEW, 1910
   Ink drawing
   Private Collection

112 MALE NUDE—BACK VIEW, 1910
   Ink drawing
   Private Collection

113 RECLINING NUDE, 1910
   Drawing, 11½ x 24 inches
   Collection Gallery of Fine Arts, Yale University

114 RECLINING WOMAN, 1910
   Drawing
   Collection Wallraf-Richartz Museum, Cologne

115 PRIESTS, 1911
   Pencil drawing
   Collection Paul J. Sachs, Cambridge

*116 NUDE RECLINING, 1911
   Ink drawing, 15 x 23½ inches
   Collection Reinhardt Galleries, New York

117 BALI STUDY, 1912
   Pencil drawing
   Private Collection, New York

118 BALINESE DANCER, 1912
   Drawing
   Collection Paul J. Sachs, Cambridge

119 DANCER, 1912
   Drawing, 19½ x 11½ inches
   Collection Mrs. W. Murray Crane, New York

120 PAGODA SCENE, 1912
   Sepia drawing, 11½ x 11¼ inches
   Collection Edward Bruce, Washington

121 WOMAN STANDING WITH BASKET ON HEAD, 1912
   Drawing
   Private Collection, New York

122 BAZAAR, BALI, 1912
   Pencil drawing, 20½ x 17 inches
   Collection The Milch Galleries, New York

123 BAZAAR, BALI, 1913
   Drawing, 21 x 16 inches
   Collection Lili Du Bois Reymond, Germany

124 FIGURE, 1913
   Pencil drawing
   Collection The Metropolitan Museum of Art, New York

125 MOTHER AND CHILD, 1913
   Pencil drawing
   Collection The Metropolitan Museum of Art, New York

126 STANDING FIGURE, 1913
   Crayon drawing, 19 x 10¼ inches
   Collection Carnegie Institute, Pittsburgh

127 BAZAAR, BALI, 1913
   Pencil drawing, 20 x 22 inches
   Collection the Artist

128 BALI MAN AND CHILDREN, 1913
   Pencil drawing, 14½ x 9 inches
   Collection the Artist

34

129 BALI WOMAN SEATED, 1913
   Pencil drawing, 22½ x 15 inches
   Collection the Artist

130 BALINESE DANCER, 1914
   Pencil drawing
   Private Collection, New York

131 GIRL WITH A BASKET, BALI, 1914
   Pencil drawing
   Collection Harold Woodbury Parsons, Boston

132 TWO GIRLS, 1914
   Pencil drawing
   Collection The Metropolitan Museum of Art, New York

133 BALI WOMAN, 1914
   Chinese ink drawing, 18 x 13 inches
   Collection Reinhardt Galleries, New York

134 MAINE ROCKS, 1916
   Ink drawing, 30 x 24½ inches (framed)
   Collection Stephan Bourgeois, New York

135 ROCK STUDY, NO. 1, 1916
   Blue crayon drawing, 16½ x 22 inches
   Collection Dr. and Mrs. Joseph Asch, New York

136 INDIAN, 1917
   Drawing
   Private Collection, New York

137 ROCKS, MONHEGAN ISLAND, 1917
   Drawing in color, 24 x 30 inches
   Collection Dr. and Mrs. Horace Kallen, New York

138 MABEL DODGE, 1917
   Sepia drawing, 23½ x 16 inches
   Collection the Artist

139 MONHEGAN ISLAND, 1917
   Chalk drawing, 23 x 17 inches
   Collection Reinhardt Galleries, New York

140 COMPOSITION, 1918
   Drawing
   Collection Frank Crowninshield, New York

141 INDIAN, 1918
   Charcoal drawing
   Collection Mrs. Frances M. Wolcott, New York

142 INDIAN MEDICINE MAN, 1918
   Drawing, 12 x 16 inches
   Collection Harry T. Lindeberg, New York

143 ROCK STUDY, NO. 2, 1918
   Drawing
   Private Collection, New York

144 ROCK STUDY, NO. 3, 1918
   Drawing
   Private Collection, New York

145 ROCKS AND WATER, 1918
   Drawing
   Private Collection, New York

146 A WAR PRISONER, 1919
   Charcoal drawing, 12 x 17½ inches
   Owned by Mr. and Mrs. George A. Spiegelberg, New York

147 GIRL'S HEAD, 1920
   Pencil drawing
   Collection Mr. and Mrs. Samuel A. Lewisohn, New York

148 NUDE, 1921
   Charcoal drawing
   Private Collection, New York

149 OX, 1922
   Sepia drawing
   Collection Harold Woodbury Parsons, Boston

150 TWO DEER, 1922
   Crayon drawing
   Collection Mrs. Alma Wertheim, New York

151 GIRL FROM ANTICOLI, 1922
   Color drawing
   Collection Wallraf-Richartz Museum, Cologne

152 GIRL, 1922
   Drawing, 25½ x 13½ inches
   Collection The Milch Galleries, New York

153 GIRL'S HEAD, 1923
   Drawing
   Collection Alex Vömel, Düsseldorf

154 ANTICOLI REAPER, 1923
   Drawing
   Collection Adolf Fischer, Düsseldorf

155 STUDY OF VERA STERNE, 1925–26
   Drawing
   Collection Mr. and Mrs. Walter Hochschild, New York

*156 VERA STERNE, 1930
   Charcoal drawing, 36 x 20 inches
   Collection Reinhardt Galleries, New York

*157 BURMESE MONKS, 1930
   Ink drawing, 17 x 22½ inches
   Collection Reinhardt Galleries, New York

*158 PAGODA GROUP, BURMA, 1930
   Ink drawing, 17 x 22½ inches
   Collection Reinhardt Galleries, New York

*159 ANTICOLI STUDY, NO. 1, 1932
   Charcoal drawing, 39¼ x 25 inches
   Collection the Artist

*160 ANTICOLI STUDY, NO. 2, 1932
   Charcoal drawing, 39¼ x 27½ inches
   Collection Reinhardt Galleries, New York

161 ANTICOLI STUDY, NO. 3, 1932
   Charcoal drawing
   Collection Reinhardt Galleries, New York

162 ANTICOLI STUDY, NO. 4, 1932
   Charcoal drawing
   Collection Reinhardt Galleries, New York

SCULPTURE

163 HEAD OF A BOMB THROWER, 1909
   Bronze, 12⅜ inches high
   Collection The Metropolitan Museum of Art, New York

*164 PUEBLO INDIAN, 1918
   Bronze, 22½ inches high
   Collection Mrs. Mabel Dodge Luhan, Taos, New Mexico

165 HEAD OF SENTA, 1919
   Bronze, 15 inches high
   Collection Adolph Lewisohn, New York

*166 THE AWAKENING, 1923–24
   Bronze, 49½ inches high, base 61½ x 26 inches
   Collection Brooklyn Museum

167 THE BOAT BUILDER, Model for Rogers-Kennedy Memorial, Worcester, Massachusetts,
   1928
   Plaster relief, 85 x 100 inches
   Collection the Artist

*168 THE PRAYER, Model for Rogers-Kennedy Memorial, Worcester, Massachusetts, 1928
   Plaster relief, 85 x 72 inches
   Collection the Artist

169 RESTING, Model for Rogers-Kennedy Memorial, Worcester, Massachusetts, 1928
   Plaster relief, 85 x 72 inches
   Collection the Artist

170 EDUCATION, Model for Rogers-Kennedy Memorial, Worcester, Massachusetts, 1928
Plaster relief, 85 x 39 inches
Collection the Artist

171 WOMAN WITH A RAKE, Model for Rogers-Kennedy Memorial, Worcester, Massachusetts, 1928
Plaster relief, 85 x 39 inches
Collection the Artist

172 HEAD OF PIONEER WOMAN, Model for Rogers-Kennedy Memorial, Worcester, Massachusetts, 1928
Plaster, 22 inches high
Collection the Artist

173 YOUNG GIRL, 1932
Plaster, 72 inches high
Collection the Artist

*174 SITTING FIGURE, 1932
Marble, 23 inches high
Collection the Artist

PLATES

20 DANCE OF THE ELEMENTS, BALI, 1913
Oil on canvas, 57 x 65 inches
Private Collection

34 TEMPLE FEAST, BALI, 1914
Oil on canvas, 39 x 42½ inches
Collection The Milch Galleries, New York

50 SACRIFICE, 1919
Oil on canvas, 46 x 39¼ inches
Collection Adolph Lewisohn, New York

57 BREAD MAKERS, 1923
Oil on canvas, 49 x 33 ¼ inches
Private Collection

58 EGGS WITH CARAFE, 1923
Oil on canvas, 16½ x 19 inches
Collection Mr. and Mrs. Samuel A. Lewisohn, New York

59 INEZ, 1923
Oil on canvas, 52½ x 40¾ inches
Collection Lord Duveen of Millbank, New York

64 AFTERNOON, 1924
Oil on canvas, 45 x 32 inches
Collection Phillips Memorial Gallery, Washington

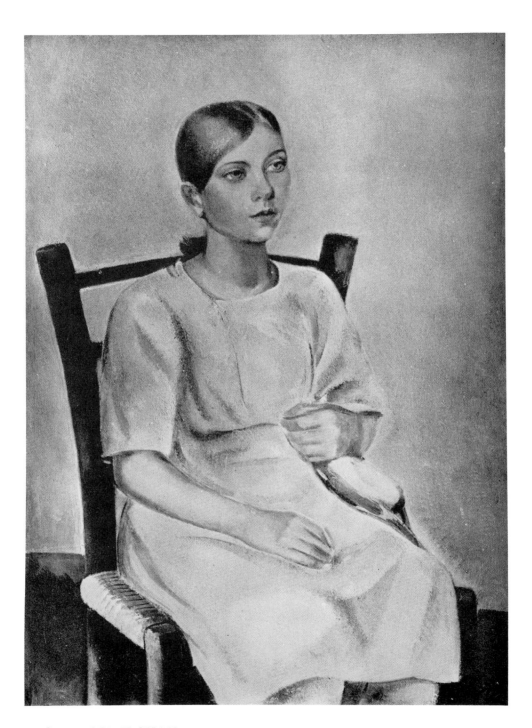

78 GIRL IN BLUE CHAIR, 1928
Oil on canvas, 34 x 24 inches
Collection Mr. and Mrs. Samuel A. Lewisohn, New York

81 THE OLD MILL, 1928
Oil on panel, 50 x 40½ inches
Collection Reinhardt Galleries, New York

93 AMERICAN IN ANTICOLI, 1932
Oil on canvas, 71 x 59 inches
Collection the Artist

94 THEME AND VARIATIONS, 1932
Oil on canvas, 50½ x 39½ inches
Collection the Artist

97 ASSUNTA, 1932
Oil on panel, 25½ x 19½ inches
Collection the Artist

105 ITALIAN BEGGAR, 1906
Drawing, 16¾ x 14¾ inches
Collection Mrs. Charles A. Robinson, Jr., Providence

116 NUDE RECLINING, 1911
Ink drawing, 15 x 23 ½ inches
Collection Reinhardt Galleries, New York

156 VERA STERNE, 1930
Charcoal drawing, 36 x 20 inches
Collection Reinhardt Galleries, New York

157 BURMESE MONKS, 1930
Ink drawing, 17 x 22½ inches
Collection Reinhardt Galleries, New York

158 PAGODA GROUP, BURMA, 1930
Ink drawing, 17 x 22½ inches
Collection Reinhardt Galleries, New York

160 ANTICOLI STUDY, NO. 2, 1932
Charcoal drawing, 39¼ x 27½ inches
Collection Reinhardt Galleries, New York

159 ANTICOLI STUDY, NO. 1, 1932
Charcoal drawing, 39¼ x 25 inches
Collection the Artist

164 PUEBLO INDIAN, 1918
Bronze, 22½ inches high
Collection Mrs. Mabel Dodge Luhan, Taos, New Mexico

166 THE AWAKENING, 1923–24
Bronze, 49½ inches high, base 61½ x 26 inches
Collection Brooklyn Museum

168 THE PRAYER, Model for Rogers-Kennedy Memorial, Worcester, Massachusetts, 1928
Plaster relief, 85 x 72 inches
Collection the Artist

174 SITTING FIGURE, 1932
Marble, 23 inches high
Collection the Artist

ONE THOUSAND COPIES OF THIS CATALOG WERE
PRINTED FOR THE TRUSTEES OF THE MUSEUM OF
MODERN ART, NEW YORK, BY PLANDOME PRESS,
NEW YORK, FEBRUARY, NINETEEN THIRTY-THREE

MUSEUM OF
MODERN ART

Stuart
Davis

by
JAMES JOHNSON SWEENEY

Acknowledgments

I wish to thank the following for their generous cooperation: Mr. Guy Pène du Bois, Mr. and Mrs. Stuart Davis, Mrs. Juliana Force, Dr. Alfred M. Frankfurter, Mr. and Mrs. Wood Gaylor, Mr. Samuel S. Goldberg, Mr. George Heard Hamilton, Mr. Henry R. Hope, Mr. Robert Laurent, Mr. Julian Levi, Romany Marie, Mrs. Raphael Navas, Mr. S. R. Naysmith, Mr. Morris S. Novik, Mr. Samuel M. Kootz, Mr. Duncan Phillips, Mr. J. de Prospo, Mrs. Irvine Schubert and Mr. and. Mrs. Burton L. Tremaine.

Grateful acknowledgment is made to Mr. Samuel Golden for his permission to quote passages from *Stuart Davis* published by the American Artists Group.

I am especially indebted to Mrs. Edith Gregor Halpert of the Downtown Gallery for her invaluable help and the use of her archives, and to Miss Margaret Miller for her assistance in preparing this book and the exhibition upon which it is based.

James Johnson Sweeney
Director of the Exhibition

Lenders

Dr. H. A. Blutman, New York; Holger Cahill, New York; Stuart Davis, New York; Mrs. Juliana Force, New York; Jan de Graaff, Portland, Ore; Mrs. Edith Gregor Halpert, New York; The Hamilton Easter Field Foundation, New York; Mr. and Mrs. John Hammond, New York; Mr. and Mrs. O'Donnell Iselin, New York; Major and Mrs. Milton L. Kramer, New York; Miss Alice D. Laughlin, New York; Mr. and Mrs. Milton Lowenthal, New York; The Miller Company, Meriden, Conn.; Municipal Broadcasting System, New York; Katherine Boutet Scallan, Chicago; Martin C. Schwab, Chicago; Estate of Herman Shulman, New York; Mr. and Mrs. Harry A. Solomon, Port Washington, N. Y.; Mr. and Mrs. Otto Spaeth, Dayton; Dr. and Mrs. Michael Watter, Philadelphia.

Indiana University, Bloomington, Ind.; Whitney Museum of American Art, New York; Phillips Memorial Gallery, Washington, D. C.; Wichita Art Museum, Wichita, Kans.; Downtown Gallery, New York.

Contents

Chronology

1894   Born Philadelphia, December 7. Father art director of the *Philadelphia Press* to which Sloan, Glackens, Luks and Shinn contributed during the nineties.

1901   Moved to East Orange, New Jersey.

1909   Entered East Orange High School.

1910   Left school to study with Robert Henri in New York. Early association with Sloan, Coleman and Glintenkamp. Exhibited with Independents.

1913   Covers and drawings for *The Masses*. Cartoonist for *Harpers Weekly*. Five watercolors in Armory Show. Left Henri School. Summer, Provincetown.

1915   Summer, Gloucester, where he returned almost yearly until 1934.

1916   Exhibited with Independents. Left *The Masses*.

1917   First one-man exhibition, Sheridan Square Gallery, New York.

1918   One-man show, Ardsley Gallery, Brooklyn. Mapmaking for Army Intelligence Department. To Havana with Coleman.

1923   Summer, New Mexico.

1925   One-man show, Newark Museum.

1927   First one-man show, Downtown Gallery.

1928   *Eggbeater* pictures; end of May to Paris.

1929   Return to New York, late August; to Gloucester. One-man show, Whitney Studio Galleries.

1930   One-man show, Downtown Galleries.

1931   Began teaching at Art Students League.

1932   Participated in Museum of Modern Art mural exhibition. Mural for Radio City Music Hall. One-man show, Downtown Gallery.

1933   Enrolled in Federal Art Project, December.

1934-   Artists Congress activities: editor of the *Art Front,* 1935; national secretary, 1936; national
1939   chairman, 1938. W.P.A. murals. Mural for New York World's Fair.

1940   Resigned from Artists Congress. Began to teach at New School for Social Research.

1941   Retrospective exhibitions: Cincinnati Modern Art Society, and Indiana University.

1943   One-man show, Downtown Gallery.

1945   Retrospective exhibition, The Museum of Modern Art.

Stuart Davis

To many people a picture is a replica of a thing, or a story about some kind of situation. To an artist, on the other hand, it is an object which has been formed by an individual in response to emotional and intellectual needs. His purpose is never to counterfeit a subject but to develop a new subject. His purpose is also to live in giving importance to certain qualities in himself, which everyone presumably possesses, but which relatively few cultivate.

This is the core of Stuart Davis' artistic beliefs. This is the line along which he has worked since his student days under Robert Henri, through the lesson of The Armory Show of 1913, to the realization of one of the most individual American pictorial idioms of our period. Humor, a responsiveness to environment, and a clear-thinking realistic outlook, in addition to his native feeling for color and compositional relationships, are the qualities which Davis has most consistently cultivated. These are the qualities which form the backbone of his work, which give it its warmth, its bluntness, its infectious vitality.

Paris School, abstraction, escapism? Nope, just color-space compositions celebrating the resolution in art of stresses set up by some aspects of the American scene.*

Stuart Davis was born in Philadelphia, December 7, 1894. His father and mother had both studied art at the Pennsylvania Academy of Fine Arts under Thomas Anschütz. At the time of Davis' birth his father, Edward Wyatt Davis, was art director of the *Philadelphia Press*. That Davis should adopt art as a profession was taken as a matter of course. *In writing autobiographical sketches it is not unusual for artists to dwell on the obstacles they had to overcome before gaining the opportunity to study. I am deprived of the profound satisfaction of recounting such a victory over stubborn opposition. I had no obstacles to overcome.*

His father originally intended to take up painting. *As a kid he traveled round the country as a sign painter. He worked for a paint company, hand lettering sign boards. As art director of the* Press *his work was mainly layout and arranging assignments for other artists. However, he frequently drew cartoons himself and was the first in Philadelphia to reproduce paintings in a newspaper directly from photographs.* Among the artists working in his department were John Sloan, George Luks, William Glackens

* In the following essay the artist as often as possible speaks for himself. Italicized text indicates statements made by the artist in interviews with the writer, excerpts from a forthcoming autobiography, articles by Davis or previously published interviews, sources of which are indicated on page 40. In all instances the quotations have been read and approved by the artist.

and Everett Shinn. These, with Robert Henri, were to form the nucleus of the group known as The Eight. Davis' father's closest friends were Sloan and Shinn. At one time he shared a studio with Shinn. Henri and Luks were also intimates of his. This was the time when Luks was doing his famous comic strip, *The Yellow Kid. Robert Henri had studied earlier at the Academy and had the means to continue his studies in Europe without interruption. On his return to Philadelphia he became, in a sense, the mentor of these artists whose painting ambitions, with the exception of Glackens', had been curtailed by the need to do newspaper illustrations and comic strips for a living.*

In the year 1901 Davis' father was appointed art editor and cartoonist on the *Newark Evening News.* The family moved from Philadelphia to East Orange, New Jersey. Shortly afterward Sloan moved to New York, followed one by one by the other members of the group. And in 1909 Henri, who had been teaching at William Chase's School in New York opened one there himself. That was Davis' first year in high school in East Orange. And before the year was over he had left and was attending Henri's classes in New York.

At Henri's School: New York, 1910-1913

The Henri School was regarded as radical and revolutionary in its methods, and it was. All the usual art school routine was repudiated. Individuality of expression was the keynote and Henri's broad point of view in his criticisms was very effective in evoking it. Art was not a matter of rules and techniques, or the search for an absolute ideal of beauty. . . . It was the expression of ideas and emotions about the life of the time. We were encouraged to make sketches of everyday life in the streets, the theatre, the restaurant and everywhere else. These were transformed into paintings in the school studios. On Saturday mornings they were all hung at the composition class. Henri talked about them, about music, about literature and life in general in a very stimulating and entertaining manner.

Two years earlier the group known as The Eight, made up principally of Davis' father's old associates on the *Philadelphia Press,* had held their first and only exhibition in the Macbeth Gallery in New York. In subject matter and to a certain degree in technique their work was a protest against the artificial "good taste" which threatened to kill any vigor in the art of the day. The group's predilection for common subjects from the world of saloons, alleyways, gutters, tramyards, night courts and the like had won them the title of the Ash Can School. But fundamentally their outlook was a reaffirmation of the strain of romantic American realism which in an earlier period and another environment had produced work like that of Mount, Bingham, Eastman Johnson and Winslow Homer.

Almost immediately on his arrival in New York, Davis had struck up an acquaintance with two slightly older painters, Henry Glintenkamp and Glenn O. Coleman. *Enthusiasm for running around and drawing things in the raw ran high. . . . Coleman, Henry Glintenkamp and myself toured extensively in metropolitan environs. Chinatown, the Bowery, the burlesque shows, the Brooklyn Bridge; McSorley's Saloon on East 7th Street; the Music Halls of Hoboken, Weehawken, Fort Lee; the Negro saloons, rides on canal boats under the Public Market and lengthy discussions with Gar Sparks, artist proprietor of a candy store—the latter all in Newark, N. J. Glintenkamp organized an art club or school in Hoboken for local Hobokenites. Hoboken at the time was still very German—very foreign due to its shipping—still unspoiled. Its saloons had all sorts of entertainment—even vaudeville. Coleman at the time was more or less my guide and counsellor. He was five years older than I was. He was not much interested in ideas—*

Cover for *The Masses.* 1913.

Negro Saloon. 1912. Watercolor, 15 x 11".
Owned by the artist.

didn't give a whoop in hell about other people's paintings. He liked life in the streets—or at least in some streets. He liked jazz. He liked drawings of the life of common people along the lines of Hogarth. Coleman was a very good painter, very talented—had no problems or psychological obstacles. He did not wonder. He felt the way he painted was the right way without knowing what the right way was, just as I knew the Negro piano players we listened to together knew how to play the piano.

In this early period of riding, walking, and gadding about all over the place, it seems a great many drawings and paintings were made. . . . Coleman and I spent much of our time listening to the Negro piano players in Newark dives. These saloons catered to the poorest Negroes and, outside of beer, the favorite drink was a glass of gin with a cherry in it which sold for five cents. The pianists were unpaid, playing for the love of art alone, and many of them were very fine. In one place the piano was covered on top and sides with barbed wire to discourage lounging on it and to give the performer more scope while at work. But the big point with us was that in all of these places you could hear a tin-pan alley tune turned into real music for the cost of a five cent beer.

Another "big point" was the influence of Henri's liberal viewpoint which had already begun to show in Davis' work, although Davis was barely sixteen. From 1910 to 1913 he continued to attend classes at Henri's school. But throughout the period he exhibited in various group shows: with the Independents in 1910; in February, 1911 at the Newark Free Public Library in a group which included Luks, Glackens, Sloan and Bellows; and in November, 1912 at the New York Water Color Club. At the same time he was designing covers for *The Masses*. With Sloan as art editor, *The Masses* had introduced a new realistic and satiric note related to the general outlook of The Eight. One of Davis' covers, that of the June, 1913 issue (p. 7), was singled out by Franklin P. Adams, then columnist of the *New York Evening Mail*, as "the best magazine cover of the year."

Henri, as Davis recalls, *was a good man at teaching.* One of Davis' *Masses* cartoons, *Saving the Corpse,* echoes clearly Henri's intransigeant attitude toward outworn tradition. *What you did not learn in Henri's School, was a useful methodology. But this had its virtues as well as its faults.*

Whatever the Henri School may have lacked in systematic discipline was more than made up for by other positive contributions. It took art off the academic pedestal and by affirming its origin in the life of the day developed a critical sense toward social values in the student. If there may have been a tendency toward anarchistic individualism, any preconceived ideas about racial, national, or class superiorities could not thrive in its atmosphere. By developing the student's confidence in his own perceptions it gave

Saving the Corpse.

Saving the Corpse. 1913. Cartoon for *The Masses.*

8

his work a freshness and personality that was lacking in the student work of other schools. On the other hand the emphasis on "anti-artistic" subject matter, which was implicit in the whole Henri idea tended to give subject matter, as such, a more important place than it deserves in art. In repudiating academic rules of picture structure, new ones suitable to the purpose were insufficiently established. The borderline between descriptive and illustrative painting and art as an autonomous sensate object was never clarified. Because of this the general purpose of making works of art that were sufficient in themselves was often defeated. Reliance on the vitality of subject matter to carry the interest prevented an objective appraisal of the dynamics of the actual color-space relations on the canvas. I became vaguely aware of this on seeing the work at The Armory Show, but it took years to clarify the point.

The Armory Show

The *International Exhibition of Modern Art*, popularly known as The Armory Show was held in February, 1913 in the armory of the Sixty-ninth Infantry in New York City. It was America's first popular introduction to the work of the vanguard European painters and sculptors. Organized exclusively by artists, its purpose was clearly stated in the foreword to its catalog:

"The American artists exhibiting here consider the exhibition as of equal importance for themselves as for the public. The less they find their work showing signs of the developments indicated in the Europeans, the more reason they will have to consider whether or not painters or sculptors here have fallen behind through escaping the incidence through distance, and for other reasons, of the forces that have manifested themselves on the other side of the Atlantic. Art is a sign of life. There can be no life without change. To be afraid of what is different is to be afraid of life. . . . This exhibition is an indication that the Association of American Painters and Sculptors is against cowardice even when it takes the form of amiable self-satisfaction."*

The exhibition was a panorama of the progressive developments of European art during the three-quarters of a century previous to 1913. There was a large American section in which Davis was represented by five watercolors, similar to *Negro Saloon* (p. 7). But it is not so much the honor of being represented in this group that Davis looks back on with such satisfaction today as the new outlook on the world of painting the exhibition gave him. It brought him suddenly face to face with what he had been looking for ever since Henri had opened his eyes to the need for self-expression: an idiom free of academicism, through which he might work out a personal pictorial logic.

The Armory Show was the greatest shock to me—the greatest single influence I have experienced in my work. All my immediately subsequent efforts went toward incorporating Armory Show ideas into my work.

It is difficult today to visualize the impact of this gigantic exhibition. Only isolated examples of the modern movement had ever been seen over here. Here indeed was the vindication of the anti-academy position of the Henri School, with developments in undreamed of directions.

I was enormously stimulated by it although appreciation of the more abstract work came later. I

* F. J. Gregg. Preface to *International Exhibition of Modern Art*. Association of American Painters and Sculptors, Inc. New York. 1913.

responded particularly to Gauguin, van Gogh and Matisse, because broad generalization of form and non-imitative use of color were already in my own experience . . . I was interested in Gauguin's arbitrary use of color rather than his exotic subject matter. In the case of van Gogh the subject matter also interested me because it was fields and things I knew. My interest in van Gogh was not solely an interest in a work of art, but in a way of expressing something I saw about me. As a result I never had the feeling that van Gogh's painting was at all alien. Cézanne and the cubists came later. It was probably an intellectual approach: not only the thing you knew but a way of thinking about the things you knew. In Gauguin, van Gogh and Matisse . . . I sensed an objective order which was lacking in my own work and which was present here without relation to any particular subject matter. It gave me the same excitement I got from the numerical precision of the Negro piano players in the Newark saloons. I resolved that I would quite definitely have to become a "modern" artist. It took an awful long time. I soon learned to think of color more or less objectively so that I could paint a green tree red without batting an eye. Purple or green faces didn't bother me at all, and I even learned to sew buttons and glue excelsior on the canvas without feeling any sense of guilt. But the ability to think about positional relationships objectively in terms of what they were, instead of what they represented, took many years.

Nevertheless the old mould was broken. From now on he could no longer return wholeheartedly to the type of work he had been producing before The Armory Show. And almost at once he set about trying to work out a new language of forms in which to express himself.

Through the publication of my work in The Masses *I received an offer in 1913 to make a full page drawing each week for* Harper's Weekly, *then being revived by Norman Hapgood. With this steady employment I set sail for Provincetown, Massachusetts. The drawings as I recall were not too hot, and the "ideas" were questionable, but they fitted in with the desired "liberal" kick on which the magazine was oriented. Provincetown was a new experience for me and made me a continuing addict of the New England coast.*

At that time Provincetown retained a considerable vestige of its former commercial reason for being. . . . Romance of the sea filled my soul. Nothing much came of it in an immediate sense, but elements in the experience served me in realizing my compulsion to be a "modern" artist. On clear days the air and water had a brilliance of light greater than I had ever seen. While this tended to destroy local color, it stimulated the desire to invent high intensity color intervals. Although my efforts were somewhat tentative, the local subject matter suited my ambition. The presence of artists and writers, not too many, added intellectual stimulus to the natural charm of the place. I met Charles Demuth, and his superior knowledge of what it was all about was a great help to me. I returned again in the following year and left in the fall with considerable reluctance.

Sloan used to rave about Gloucester. In 1915 I went there on his recommendation. That was the place I had been looking for. It had the brilliant light of Provincetown, but with the important additions to topographical severity and the architectural beauties of the Gloucester schooner. The schooner is a very necessary element in coherent thinking about art. I do not refer to its own beauty of form, but to the fact that its masts define the often empty sky expanse. They function as a color-space coordinate between earth and sky. They make it possible for the novice landscape painter to evade the dangers of "taking off" into the void as soon as his eye hits the horizon. From the masts of schooners the artist eventually learns to invent his own coordinates, when for some unavoidable reason they are not present.

10

Gloucester Terrace. 1916. Oil on canvas, 38 x 30". Owned by the artist.

In spite, however, of The Armory Show's revelation of the picture as a reality in itself, not merely a replica of a visual expression, Davis' illustrative work for *The Masses* continued to hold him more or less to the sociological realist approach of The Eight. And in the spring of 1915 we find him represented in the first *American Salon of Humorists* in the Folsom Gallery in New York.

But in February of the following year a split took place among the editors of *The Masses* on the issue of "art vs. ideas." Sloan, Glintenkamp, Coleman, Robert Carlton Brown and Davis took one side, and Max Eastman, Floyd Dell, John Reed and Art Young took the other. Eastman felt that many of the subscribers could not understand the art *The Masses* published unless it was explained by captions. Art

Yellow Hills. 1919. Oil on canvas, 23⅜ x 29¼″. Downtown Gallery.

Young stated in a press interview at the time that "the five dissenting artists want to run pictures of ash cans and girls hitching up their skirts in Horatio Street—regardless of ideas—and without title. . . . On the other hand a group of us believe that such pictures belong better in exclusive art magazines. For my part I do not care to be connected with a publication that does not try to point the way out of a sordid materialistic world."*

The Eastman party won hands down. John Sloan and his friends resigned. As Davis remarks, *Apparently the battle between "pure art" and an "art of ideas" is not merely a contemporary manifestation.* Thanks to the seed planted by The Armory Show, Davis had already begun to feel that art had its own reason for existence—that it should never be content with a supporting role. The break with *The Masses* merely confirmed him in his resolve to pursue his search for free self-expression.

* New York Sun. April 8, 1916.

In a painting such as *Gloucester Terrace* of 1916 (p. 11) the new direction is apparent. The color is evidently inspired by the artist's mood or emotions at the time of painting rather than by visual experience; and his *Yellow Hills* is admittedly van Gogh applied to the Pennsylvania countryside.

In December, 1917 Davis had his first one-man show at the Sheridan Square Gallery in New York; and in the spring of 1918 another was given him at the Ardsley Gallery in Brooklyn.

During the closing months of the last war, Davis served in a branch of the Army Intelligence Department. A special commission had been set up under Walter Lippmann to prepare materials for the peace conference. Davis' work was mainly drafting maps and graphs along ethnographic lines. In the Spanish influenza epidemic towards the close of 1918 he was severely stricken. To recuperate he went with Coleman to Havana. On his return he divided his time between Gloucester and New York until 1923. Ideas and points of view that were new to American painters in The Armory Show in 1913 had by this time become considerably more familiar. Alfred Stieglitz in his "291" exhibitions and Miss Katherine Dreier's *Société Anonyme* had done much to carry on the work initiated by Arthur B. Davies, Walt Kuhn, Walter Pach and their fellow members of the Association of American Painters and Sculptors. Since 1915 many important French artists such as Marcel Duchamp, Francis Picabia, Jacques Villon and others had settled in New York and had become familiar figures in the Lincoln Arcade next to which Davis and Glintenkamp had their studio at 1931 Broadway. Work such as Picabia's *Le Midi*, with its palm trees done in macaroni and feathers,* made it easier for Davis "to sew buttons and glue excelsior on the canvas without feeling any sense of guilt." Cubist *papiers collés,* or pasted paper compositions, had brought home the compositional value of large color areas after cubism's break-up of conventional forms. Through them the cubists had reasserted the two-dimensional character of the canvas and had called attention to the pictorial value of contrasted textures. Davis had picked up all these hints from his European exemplars. But when he followed them to the next stage—the simulation of *papiers collés* in oil—we find him imitating newstype and cigarette trademarks with a meticulous illusionism and precision of detail that is perhaps more native, in its resemblance to the work of the ninetenth-century American painter William Harnett, than it is cubist (p. 14).

Still there is already a hint of Léger's influence in Davis' work. In these compositions he was attempting to eliminate softness of tone, vagueness of contour, grayness in color and to organize his contrasts more dynamically than most of his American contemporaries were doing. A few years later definite similarities of conception are recognizable between his *Apple and Jug* of 1923 and Léger's work of the same period, such as *Le Siphon*. Léger in his feeling for austere simplicity had reacted from the soft grace of some of his cubist colleagues' work. Davis recognized in Léger's work interests similar to his own, a response to the age of things, speed, loud noises, black headlines. As he was to say later, "Léger is the most American painter painting today."

In the work of these years the elements of Davis' painting remained representational, but their organization became more and more obviously dictated by pictorial logic rather than by natural arrangement. At the same time his interest in the picture as a reflection of the natural world grew proportionately less.

* At present in the *Société Anonyme* Collection, Yale University.

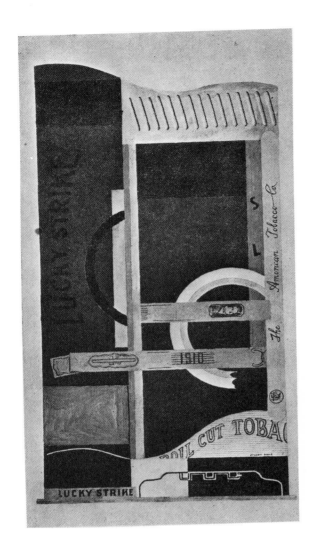

Lucky Strike. 1921. Oil on canvas, 33⅛ x 18″.
Owned by the artist.

Cigarette Papers. 1921. Watercolor on canvas,
19 x 14″. Owned by the artist.

14

Two Trees. 1925. Oil on canvas, 19 x 22". Whitney Museum of American Art.

New Mexico; Gloucester and New York; 1923-1927

Just as John Sloan used to rave about Gloucester, and I went there on his recommendation, it was the same about New Mexico—but with a difference. I spent three or four months there in 1923—until late fall—but did not do much work because the place itself was so interesting. I don't think you could do much work there except in a literal way, because the place is always there in such a dominating way. You always have to look at it. Then there's the great dead population. You don't see them but you stumble over them. A piece of pottery here and there and everywhere. It's a place for an ethnologist not an artist. Not sufficient intellectual stimulus. Forms made to order, to imitate. Colors—but I never went there again.

As Davis turned away from an interest in imitating nature, a change began to take place even in his manner of working.

From New Mexico I went to Gloucester, then oscillated from New York to Gloucester during the next few years. My family had a place there. That meant I had a place to go and Gloucester itself pleased me very much. I still think it the best place on the Atlantic Coast. . . . I used to wander over the rocks with a sketching easel, large canvases and a pack on my back looking for things to paint. Things began to go a little better, and some things I produced gave me a certain amount of satisfaction. After a number of years the idea began to dawn on me that packing and unpacking all this junk, in addition to toting it all over the Cape, was irrelevant to my purpose. I became convinced that this was definitely doing things the hard way. Following this revelation my daily sorties were unencumbered except by a small sketch book

15

of the lightest design known and a specially constructed Duralumin fountain pen. There may have been a bit of backsliding by the inclusion of a box of colored crayons, but I soon put a stop to that. The decision was a good one. . . . . It came to the point where I actually began to like the pictures I made following it. It seemed that in all this tramping around with full equipment I had actually learned something. All that was required to cash in on some of this information was to stop lifting things up and putting them down. I have scrupulously followed this discipline ever since. While I cannot recall the exact date of this revolutionary discovery, it didn't come a moment too soon.

In abandoning the weighty apparatus of the outdoor painter I did not abandon nature as subject matter. My studio pictures were all made from drawings made directly from nature. As I had learned in painting out-of-doors to use a conceptual instead of an optical perspective, so in my studio compositions I brought drawings of different places and of different things into a single focus. The necessity to select and define the spatial limits of these separate drawings, in relation to the unity of the whole picture, developed an objective attitude toward positional relations. Having already achieved this to a degree in relations of color, the two had to be integrated and thought about simultaneously. The abstract kick was on, and a different set of headaches made their appearance.

The Eggbeater Series, 1927-1928

Gradually Davis had been realizing his ambition, inspired by The Armory Show, to become a "modern" artist. From Gauguin's and van Gogh's arbitrary colors and running contour patterns he had turned to the structural simplifications of Cézanne and the post-cubist work of Léger and Picasso. In *Two Trees* of 1925 (p. 15) and *Super Table* of the same year we see an evident interest in space-organization through the ordering of the planes.

The first culmination of these efforts occurred in 1927 and 1928 when I nailed an electric fan, a rubber glove and an eggbeater to a table and used them as my exclusive subject matter for a year.

Sometimes a person gets tired of painting landscapes. Then he paints people. Sometimes he gets tired of painting people then he paints landscapes. And sometimes an uninteresting subject may be as stimulating as an interesting one. One day I set up an eggbeater in my studio and got so interested in it that I nailed it on a table and kept it there to paint. I called the pictures Eggbeater, number such and such, because it was from the eggbeater that the pictures took their impulse (p. 17).

The pictures themselves are not decorations. They are pictures. Their subject is an invented series of planes which was interesting to the artist. They were then drawn in perspective and light and shade in the same way another artist draws the planes of a human head or a landscape. They were a bit on the severe side, but the ideas involved in their construction have continued to serve me.

In fact this eggbeater series was very important for me because in this period I got away from naturalistic forms. I invented these geometrical elements. What led to it was probably my working on a single still life for a year, not wandering about the streets. Gradually through this concentration I focused on the logical elements. They became the foremost interest and the immediate and accidental aspects of the still life took second place.

The pictures that immediately preceded the eggbeater series, those of 1924 and 1925 were all based on the same idea; a generalization of form in which the subject was conceived as a series of planes and

16

Eggbeater #1. 1928. Oil on canvas, 27 x 38⅛″. Phillips Memorial Gallery.

the planes as geometrical shapes—a valid view of the structure of any subject. I had come to feel that what was interesting in a subject or what had really caused our response to it could be best expressed in a picture if these geometrical planes were arranged in direct relationship to the canvas as a flat surface. I felt that a subject had its emotional reality fundamentally through our awareness of such planes and their spatial relationships. In paintings like Super Table *the major relationships—the larger generalizations—were established, but the minor features were still imitative. In the eggbeater series, on the other hand, I made an effort to use the same method throughout. This I felt would give the picture a more objective coherence. The result was the elimination of a number of particularized optical truths which I had formerly concerned myself with. In effecting this elimination, however, the subject was not repudiated in favor of some ideal order; but this approach was regarded as a more intense means of equating the sensible material one responds to in various subjects. My aim was not to establish a self-sufficient system to take the place of the immediate and the accidental, but . . . to strip a subject down to the real physical source of its stimulus.*

I did not regard it, however, as the future aspect of all my painting, but rather as a groping towards a structural concept. So when I went to Paris, a few months later, the same structural approach remained

17

in paintings like the Rue des Rats *with more or less literal references, which to my mind did not conflict with the structural approach. In other words I did not think that particular truth eliminated general truth or general truth particular truth. I try to think of them as one thing. So you may say that everything I have done since has been based on that eggbeater idea. I have just tried to carry the idea into greater particularity without abandoning the general scope which interested me there.*

Paris, 1928-1929

In May, 1928 Mrs. Juliana R. Force of the then Whitney Studio Club bought several of my pictures. Having heard it rumored at one time or another that Paris was a good place to be, I lost no time in taking the hint. With one suitcase I hopped a boat and arrived in the center of art and culture in the middle of June. I also brought along a packing case containing my eggbeater paintings.

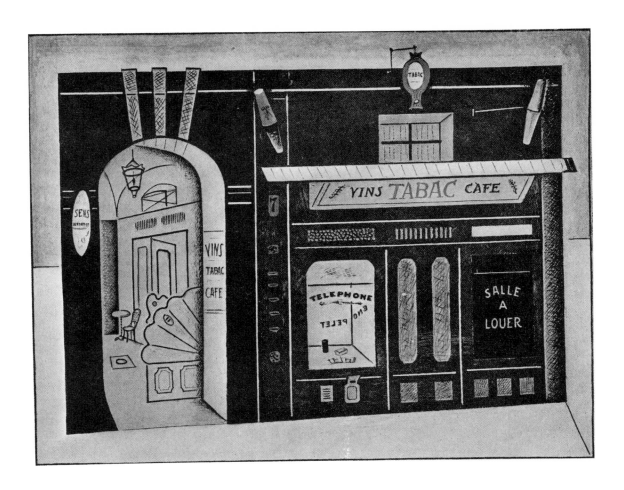

Café, Place des Vosges. 1929. Oil on canvas, 29 x 36¼". Collection Mrs. Edith Gregor Halpert.

18

Rue de l'Echaudé. 1928. Oil on canvas, 23⅝ x 36¼". Collection Mr. and Mrs. Otto Spaeth.

The rumors were correct. Although I did not speak a word of French I felt immediately at home. The conviction was already established on the train from Le Havre that I had done the right thing in coming to this place.

Everything about the place struck me as being just about right. I had the feeling that this was the best place in the world for an artist to live and work; and at the time it was. The prevalence of the sidewalk café was an important factor. It provided easy access to one's friends and gave extra pleasure to long walks through various parts of the city. . . . It reminded me of Philadelphia. I remembered Philadelphia only as a child . . . an old fashioned place. Paris was old fashioned, but modern as well. That was the wonderful part of it. . . . There was so much of the past and the immediate present brought together on one plane that nothing seemed left to be desired. There was a timelessness about the place that was conducive to the kind of contemplation essential to art. And the scale of the architecture was human.

And there was no feeling of being isolated from America. At one time or another I met practically every one I had ever known. Bob and Rose Brown of The Masses *days arrived from Brazil via China with forty trunks. I immediately got in touch with Elliot Paul, a Gloucester writer friend. He had lived there for several years and gave me a personally conducted tour of the sights. Paul Gaulois, artist-*

Place Pasdeloup. 1928. Oil on canvas, 36⅛ x 28½". Whitney Museum
of American Art.

restauranteur, strolled the boulevards. Niles Spencer introduced me to Hilaire Hiler, who in turn played the first Earl Hines record I ever heard. These and a hundred other amiable associations made the absence of plumbing in my studio a matter of no importance. It was a primitive life: I cooked on an alcohol burner. But I worked a lot. . . .

The year before, in New York, I had looked at my eggbeater so long that I finally had no interest in it. I stared at it until it became just a combination of planes. But over there, in Paris, the actuality was so interesting I found a desire to paint it just as it was. I had no idea, however, of wanting to stay over

20

Summer Landscape. 1930. Oil on canvas, 29 x 42″. Museum of Modern Art, Purchase Fund.

there. The very thing that made it interesting to me—the slowed-down tempo—made it monotonous. Having been born over here, with all this going on around you, you have a need for it. I didn't do anything there but paint and walk around the streets.

The anonymous forms in his eggbeater series of the year before had now given way to depictions of Paris streets that had a definite sentiment about them. They are distillations of the mood which he described Paris as having awakened in him. But they are this and something else. He had carried his eggbeater series with him to Paris in more ways than one. His Paris street scenes (pp. 18 and 19) have a structural sophistication under their lyric freshness which he could not have achieved before. His palette was clearly influenced by the Paris sunlight and the delicate tones and contrasting dark notes of the street façades of the city. But where the contrasts among the compositional elements were hard and crude in his American work of the early twenties, there is now a mellowness of surface even when he mixes sand with his paint or makes use of the broadest palette-knife modeling. The whole is drenched in light which unifies the composition. And the result is paintings such as *Place des Vosges #2* or *Rue de l'Echaudé* (p. 19), mature personal expressions deeply rooted in the artist's emotional response to the Paris urban milieu.

House and Street. 1931. Oil on canvas, 26 x 42¼". Whitney Museum of American Art.

Return from Europe, 1929

I came back to this country in August, 1929 on the maiden voyage of the Bremen. On my arrival in New York I was appalled and depressed by its giantism. Everything in Paris was human size, here everything was inhuman. It was difficult to think either of art or oneself as having any significance whatever in the face of this frenetic commercial engine. I thought "Hell, you can't do any painting here." It is partly true. But on the other hand as an American I had the need for the impersonal dynamics of New York City.

Once away from the insistence of the Paris environment, Davis felt free to return to his still-life explorations, and in *Eggbeater #5* (opposite), begun a few months after his return from Europe in 1929, we see an interest in the art of Paris as well as in the city itself. French painting had assuredly left its mark. But a personalization of this influence is also clear. In its black and white treatment and in the drawing of its forms it stands apart from the work of Picasso, Braque or Léger. At the same time if it is less seductive than *Place des Vosges #2* and *Place Pasdeloup* (p. 20), it gives the impression of greater assurance and makes a bolder use of tonal contrasts than even the most successful of his Paris work.

For Davis the art of contemporary Paris was the main life stream. It was not simply a regional expression, but the source to which all painters should go. Still the artist must never allow his roots to

22

Eggbeater #5. 1930. Oil on canvas, 50⅛ x 32¼″. The Museum of Modern Art, Purchase Fund.

New York-Paris #1. 1931. Oil on canvas, 38¼ x 51″. Downtown Gallery.

leave his native soil. His view is essentially that of T. S. Eliot, "neither in a complete uniformity, nor in an isolated self-sufficiency, can culture flourish, . . . a local and a general culture are so far from being in conflict that they are truly necessary to each other . . . uniformity means the obliteration of culture, and . . . self-sufficiency means death by starvation."* As Davis expresses it: *I am an American, born in Philadelphia of American stock. I studied art in America. I paint what I see in America, in other words, I paint the American scene. . . . I don't want people to copy Matisse or Picasso, although it is entirely proper to admit their influence. I don't make paintings like theirs. I make paintings like mine. I want to paint and do paint particular aspects of this country which interest me. But I use, as a great many others do, some of the methods of modern French painting which I consider to have universal validity. . . . Why should an American artist today be expected to be oblivious to European thought when Europe is a hundred times closer to us than it ever was before? If a Scotchman is working on television, do*

* T. S. Eliot. "The Man of Letters and the Future of Europe." *The Sewanee Review*, Summer, 1945, Vol. LIII, No. 3, pp. 336-337.

23

Sail Loft. 1930. Oil on canvas, 15¾ x 19¾". Collection Mr. and Mrs.
O'Donnell Iselin.

Cigarette Papers. 1933. Oil on composition board, 12 x
12⅜". Collection Holger Cahill.

Salt Shaker. 1931. Oil on canvas, 49⅞ x 32″. Collection Mrs. Edith Gregor Halpert.

similarly interested American inventors avoid all information as to his methods? . . . I did not spring into the world fully equipped to paint the kind of pictures I want to paint. It was therefore necessary to ask people for advice. After leaving the direct influence of Mr. Henri I sought other sources of information and, as the artists whose work I admired were not personally available, I tried to find out what they were thinking about by looking at their pictures. Chief among those consulted were Aubrey Beardsley, Toulouse-Lautrec, Seurat, Fernand Léger and Picasso.

One striking difference, however, between Davis' work and that of the Parisian leaders is an increment of humor—a playfulness in which he is perhaps closer to artists of his own generation, such as the Catalan Joan Miro, or the American Alexander Calder, than to the older men whom he has studied and admired. Davis' humor is a muscular humor, not a drawing-room wit. It is a male humor with a strand of sentiment running through it. Paris was an esthetic interlude. New York and Gloucester were Davis' native pastures. They are the fields in which he is most at ease and expresses himself most gayly. And in

Cape Ann Landscape. 1938. Oil on canvas, 20 x 30¼". Collection Mr. and Mrs. Harry A. Solomon.

26

Swing Landscape. 1938. Oil on canvas, 7 x 14'. Indiana University, on extended loan from the Federal Art Project.

the summer following his return from abroad we see him going back to his American inspiration in *Summer Landscape* (p. 21), *Jefferson Market* and *House and Street* (p. 22).

In *Summer Landscape* there is an adaptation of the idiom of *Place Pasdeloup* to a Massachusetts seaport town. The technical approach is similar; though the emphasis on perpendiculars and the repetition of jagged angles convey an impression of activity and sharpness quite different from the easy serenity of his Paris scene. In the lower half of *Jefferson Market* and especially in *House and Street* there are evidences of Fernand Léger's contrasts of unmodeled areas of local color and an emphasis on the angular machine forms. Still, in both there is a sense of locale which is never or very rarely present in Léger's work. And the locale of Davis' painting is recognizably urban New York.

The transition, however, was not effected without definite nostalgic glances. And his *New York-Paris* compositions tell the story in their combination of associational motives related to both environments. For in spite of the seeming jumble of representational elements in Davis' paintings he feels that *a picture must tell a story.* But "story" in Davis' sense goes deeper than illustrational narrative. *This story can have pictorial existence only through the artist's concept of form.*

There are an infinite number of form concepts available. My own is very simple and is based on the assumption that space is continuous and matter is discontinuous. In my formal concept . . . I never ask the question: Does this picture have depth or is it flat? I consider such a question irrelevant. I consider form (matter) as existing in space in terms of linear direction. It follows then that the forms of the subject are analyzed in terms of angular variation from successive bases of directional radiation. The

27

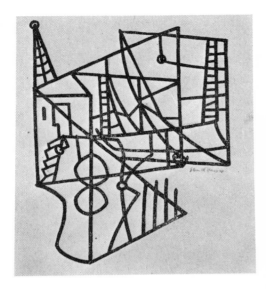

Landscape. 1932 and 1935. Oil on canvas,
25 x 22". Owned by the artist.

Shapes of Landscape Space. 1939. Oil on canvas, 36 x
28". Private collection.

phenomena of color, size, shape and texture are the result of such angular variation. And Davis' adaptation and personalization of Picasso's example on the basis of this point of view is especially well illustrated by his *Salt Shaker* (p. 25) of 1931.

1932-1939, W.P.A. and Artists Congress

In 1932 Davis went again to Gloucester. He painted his large mural *Men without Women* there for Radio City Music Hall in New York. But serious economic difficulties had begun to set in and, at the same time, illness. He came back to New York and went to a hospital. The following year he rented a room on 14th Street near 8th Avenue and took seven or eight pupils. Teaching mornings and afternoons, he had little free time for his own work.

28

Bass Rocks #2. 1939. Oil on canvas, 33 x 43". Wichita Art Museum, Murdock Collection.

In July he moved to Gloucester and remained there till December, painting several smaller pictures such as *Cigarette Papers* (p. 24). But as he recalls *Everything went to Hell. Came back to New York on Christmas Day. Made a bee-line for McSorley's Saloon. Found it closed—which made me feel very bad. Edward Bruce at the time was getting his Federal Art Project under way. I heard about it. And since I scarcely had a cent in my pockets and very slim prospects, a couple of days later I got on his payroll.*

In 1934 I became socially conscious as everyone else was doing in those days and became mixed up with the Artists Congress. This meant meetings, articles, picket lines, internal squabbles. Everything was hectic. Lots of work was done, but little painting.

Meanwhile the first Art Project folded up. Then the W.P.A. project started. Cahill came in one hot night. He had been asked to take charge. We adjourned to the saloon across the way. I encouraged him to do it at once. And I told him I wanted to get on it at once.

29

The Artists Congress had been taking all my time and energy. People came tramping in day and night. Painting had been having little chance. The Art Project was a life-saver. I made some small pictures for them. And eventually two murals: Swing Landscape (p. 27) *now at the University of Indiana, and another for Studio B, WNYC.*

Return to Easel Painting, 1939

This business of the Artists Congress and the Art Project seemed to go on for years. My pauper status continued excellent. Then suddenly I was out without a cent. I was eliminated from the Project because my five years legal period of tenure had expired. Having no money I did the conventional thing—I hired myself a studio and devoted myself to painting. I felt it was "now or never." I made Bass Rocks. *And all my recent paintings have been done here in this same studio.*

In spite, however, of all the work Davis did during the six years for the Artists Congress and the five for the Federal Art Project and the W.P.A., he succeeded in producing several easel paintings which are important in his development, notably *Cape Ann Landscape* (p. 26) and *Gloucester Harbor.* And his style, which in 1932 still retained a marked interest in Léger's oppositions of flat areas of local tone, had in the interim achieved a much greater freedom.

Mural for Studio B, WNYC. 1939. Oil on canvas, 7 x 11′. Municipal Broadcasting System.

30

Report from Rockport. 1940. Oil on canvas, 24 x 30″. Collection Mr. and Mrs. Milton Lowenthal.

Bass Rocks represents the color and space harmonies which I observed in a landscape subject. It is not a picture of every day visual aspects; it is a selection of certain relations of spatial order and logic which were actually present in the subject. Casual observation of the scene from which they were taken would not reveal the elements from which the picture was made. These harmonies only became apparent after careful study and contemplation of it (p. 29).

While Davis' pre-Art Project canvases, such as his New York-Paris series, were essentially compositions of simplified independent illustrative elements, related by contrasts of color and associational significance, in work like *Bass Rocks #2* forms were reduced to the barest linear indices and compositional unity was achieved through their interplay and an over-all color harmony.

Davis has a habit of returning to pictorial problems he had set himself in earlier stages of his development. This gives him an opportunity to test the effectiveness of the new means he has fashioned for himself as well as an opportunity for self-criticism. Already in his drawings of 1932 he had shown an interest in broad linear emphases and simplified forms. Some of these he translated into oils such as *Landscape*. And if we compare this composition with *Shapes of Landscape Space* (p. 28) we can see how he had modified his earlier drawing style and was turning to broader harmonic color areas. The main step of breaking up the lines into the smaller motives of *Bass Rocks* is not yet evident. But in *New York under Gaslight* of 1941 (p. 33) there is already evidence of the new attention to minor representational details, or particularities of the composition, as he calls them, in contradistinction to the broad generalities that were to characterize his work following *Bass Rocks*.

In *Report from Rockport* (p. 31) there are as many representational source elements as in his *New York-Paris #1* (p. 23). But since 1931 he has become steadily more interested in bringing the minor details of his picture to the same degree of amplification as the major lines of the composition. Conse-

Hot Still-Scape for Six Colors. 1940. Oil on canvas, 36 x 45″. Collection Jan de Graaff.

32

Ursine Park. 1942. Oil on canvas, 20 x 40⅛". Downtown Gallery.

Catalog of the Exhibition

In dimensions height precedes width. An asterisk (*) before the title indicates that the work is illustrated.

Self-portrait. 1912. Oil on canvas, 32 x 26⅛". Lent by the artist.

* Negro Saloon. 1912. Watercolor, 15 x 11". Lent by the artist. *Ill. p. 7.*

* Gloucester Terrace. 1916. Oil on canvas, 38 x 30". Lent by the artist. *Ill. p. 11.*

Rockport Beach. 1916. Oil on canvas, 30 x 24". Lent by the artist.

Gloucester Street. 1916. Oil on canvas, 24 x 30". Lent by the artist.

* Yellow Hills. 1919. Oil on canvas, 23⅜ x 29¼". Lent by the Downtown Gallery, New York. *Ill. p. 12.*

* Lucky Strike. 1921. Oil on canvas, 33⅛ x 18". Lent by the artist. *Ill. p. 14.*

* Cigarette Papers. 1921. Watercolor on canvas, 19 x 14". Lent by the artist. *Ill. p. 14.*

Bull Durham. 1921. Oil and watercolor on canvas, 30 x 15". Lent by the artist.

Apples and Jug. 1923. Oil on cardboard, 22 x 17⅞". Lent by the artist.

* Two Trees. 1925. Oil on canvas, 19 x 22". Lent by the Whitney Museum of American Art, New York. *Ill. p. 15.*

Super Table. 1925. Oil on canvas, 48⅛ x 34⅛". Lent by the Downtown Gallery, New York.

* Eggbeater #1. 1928. Oil on canvas, 27 x 38⅛". Lent by the Phillips Memorial Gallery, Washington, D. C. *Ill. p. 17.*

Eggbeater #3. 1928. Oil on canvas, 25 x 39". Lent by the artist.

Place des Vosges #2. 1928. Oil on canvas, 25⅝ x 36¼". Lent by Major and Mrs. Milton L. Kramer, New York.

* Rue de l'Echaudé. 1928. Oil on canvas, 23⅝ x 36¼". Lent by Mr. and Mrs. Otto Spaeth, Dayton, Ohio. *Ill. p. 19.*

Blue Café. 1928. Oil on canvas, 18½ x 21⅝". Lent by the Phillips Memorial Gallery, Washington, D. C.

Rue des Rats #1. 1928. Oil on canvas, 23⅝ x 36¼". Lent by the Estate of Herman Shulman, New York.

* Place Pasdeloup. 1928. Oil on canvas, 36⅛ x 28½". Lent by the Whitney Museum of American Art, New York. *Ill. p. 20.*

Hôtel de France. 1928. Oil on canvas, 28¾ x 23½". Lent by Martin C. Schwab and Katherine Boutet Scallan, Chicago.

* Café, Place des Vosges. 1929. Oil on canvas, 29 x 36¼". Lent by Mrs. Edith Gregor Halpert, New York. *Ill. p. 18.*

Arch-Hôtel. 1929. Oil on canvas, 28½ x 39¼". Lent by the artist.

Interior. 1930. Oil on canvas, 24⅛ x 20⅛". Lent by Dr. and Mrs. Michael Watter, Philadelphia.

* Sail Loft. 1930. Oil on canvas, 15¾ x 19¾". Lent by Mr. and Mrs. O'Donnell Iselin, New York. *Ill. p. 24.*

* Eggbeater #5. 1930. Oil on canvas, 50⅛ x 32¼". The Museum of Modern Art, Purchase Fund. *Color plate, opp. p. 22.*

* Summer Landscape. 1930. Oil on canvas, 29 x 42". The Museum of Modern Art, Purchase Fund. *Ill. p. 21.*

Still Life with Flowers. 1930. Oil on canvas, 40 x 32". Lent by the Downtown Gallery, New York.

Jefferson Market. 1930. Oil on canvas, 34 x 23". Lent by the Downtown Gallery, New York.

* New York-Paris #1. 1931. Oil on canvas, 38¼ x 51". Lent by the Downtown Gallery, New York. *Ill. p. 23.*

New York-Paris #2. 1931. Oil on canvas, 30 x 40". Lent by the Hamilton Easter Field Foundation, New York.

* House and Street. 1931. Oil on canvas, 26 x 42¼". Lent by the Whitney Museum of American Art, New York. *Ill. p. 22.*

* Salt Shaker. 1931. Oil on canvas, 49⅞ x 32". Lent by Mrs. Edith Gregor Halpert, New York. *Ill. p. 25.*

Composition with Winch. 1931. Oil on canvas, 22¼ x 27". Lent by Dr. H. A. Blutman, New York.

The Red Cart. 1932. Oil on canvas, 32⅛ x 50". Lent by Miss Alice D. Laughlin, New York.

* Cigarette Papers. 1933. Oil on composition board, 12 x 12⅜". Lent by Holger Cahill, New York. *Ill. p. 24.*

* Landscape. 1932 and 1935. Oil on canvas, 25 x 22″. Lent by the artist. *Ill. p. 28.*

Sunrise. 1933. Oil on canvas, 10 x 14″. Lent by Holger Cahill, New York.

Composition #3. c. 1934. Ink drawing, 21¼ x 29¾″. The Museum of Modern Art, gift of Mrs. John D. Rockefeller, Jr.

* Cape Ann Landscape. 1938. Oil on canvas, 20 x 30¼″. Lent by Mr. and Mrs. Harry A. Solomon. Port Washington, N. Y. *Ill. p. 26.*

Gloucester Harbor. 1938. Oil on canvas, 23 x 30″. Lent by Mr. and Mrs. John Hammond, New York.

* Swing Landscape. 1938. Oil on canvas, 7 x 14′. Lent by Indiana University, Bloomington, Ind. *Ill. p. 27.*

* Shapes of Landscape Space. 1939. Oil on canvas, 36 x 28″. Lent anonymously. *Ill. p. 28*

* Bass Rocks #2. 1939. Oil on canvas, 33 x 43″. Lent by the Wichita Art Museum, Murdock Collection, Wichita, Kansas. *Ill. p. 29.*

Radio Tube. c. 1939. Gouache, 22 x 14¾″. Lent by Mrs. Juliana Force, New York.

* Mural for Studio B, WNYC. 1939. Oil on canvas, 7 x 11′. Lent by the Municipal Broadcasting System, New York. *Ill. p. 30.*

Study for Hot Still-Scape. 1940. Oil on canvas, 9 x 12″. The Museum of Modern Art, given anonymously.

* Hot Still-Scape for Six Colors. 1940. Oil on canvas, 36 x 45″. Lent by Jan de Graaff, Portland, Ore. *Ill. p. 32.*

* Report from Rockport. 1940. Oil on canvas, 24 x 30″. Lent by Mr. and Mrs. Milton Lowenthal, New York. *Ill. p. 31.*

* New York under Gaslight. 1941. Oil on canvas, 32 x 45″. Lent by the Estate of Herman Shulman, New York. *Ill. p. 33.*

* Ursine Park. 1942. Oil on canvas, 20 x 40⅛″. Lent by the Downtown Gallery, New York. *Color plate, opp. p. 34.*

* Arboretum by Flashbulb. 1942. Oil on canvas, 18 x 36″. Lent by Mr. and Mrs. Milton Lowenthal, New York. *Ill. p. 34.*

Flying Carpet. 1942. Wool rug, woven by V'Soske. 7′ 1″ x 10′. The Museum of Modern Art, Edgar J. Kaufmann, Jr. Fund.

* For Internal Use Only. 1945. Oil on canvas, 48 x 24″. Lent by the Miller Company, Meriden, Conn. *Color frontispiece.*

Work by Davis in American Public Collections

BLOOMINGTON, IND. Indiana University
1 mural
Extended loan from the Federal Art Project.

BLOOMFIELD HILLS, MICH. Cranbrook Museum
1 oil

BUFFALO, N. Y. Albright Art Gallery
1 oil

HANOVER, N. H. Dartmouth College
1 gouache

LEXINGTON, KY. University of Kentucky
1 lithograph

LOS ANGELES, CALIF. Los Angeles Museum, Preston Harrison Collection
1 watercolor

MILWAUKEE, WIS. Milwaukee Art Institute
1 oil

NEWARK, N. J. Newark Museum
1 oil
3 watercolors

NEWARK, N. J. Newark Free Public Library
1 lithograph

NEW YORK, N. Y. Museum of Modern Art
3 oils
1 gouache
1 rug
2 drawings
7 lithographs

NEW YORK, N. Y. Whitney Museum of American Art
5 oils
3 gouaches
2 drawings

PHILADELPHIA, PENN. Pennsylvania Academy of Fine Arts
1 oil

PITTSBURGH, PENN. Carnegie Institute
1 lithograph

SAN DIEGO, CALIF. San Diego Museum
1 oil

TUCSON, ARIZ. University of Arizona.
1 oil

WASHINGTON, D. C. Library of Congress
lithographs

WASHINGTON, D. C. Phillips Memorial Gallery
5 oils

WICHITA, KANS. Wichita Art Museum
1 oil

Prints by Davis

LITHOGRAPHS ON STONE

Hôtel de France. 1928. 11½ x 14¾″. 30 imprs.

Place des Vosges. 1928. 9⅝ x 13⅞″. 10 imprs.

Adit. 1928. 10¼ x 11⅞″. 10 imprs.

Rue de l'Echaudé. 1929. 9⅞ x 14¾″. 30 imprs.

Arch. 1929. 9¾ x 13⅝″. 30 imprs.

Arch #2. 1929. 10¼ x 13¾″. 30 imprs.

*Au Bon Coin. 1929. 8⅜ x 10⅝″. 30 imprs.

Hôtel-Café. 1929. 8⅜ x 10⅝″. 30 imprs.

Place Pasdeloup #1. 1929. 11½ x 14⅜″. 10 imprs.

*Place Pasdeloup #2. 1929. 11⅜ x 14⅜″. 20 imprs.

Rue des Rats. 1929. 10½ x 15½″. 30 imprs.

LITHOGRAPHS ON ZINC

*Two Heads. 1930. 10¾ x 13¼″. 12 imprs.

*Barber Shop Chord. 1931. 14 x 19″. 25 imprs.

*Composition. 1931. 9 x 10″. 25 imprs.

*Sixth Avenue El. 1931. 12 x 17⅞″. 25 imprs.

Sixth Avenue El #2. 1931. 11 x 15⅛″. 25 imprs.

Theatre on the Beach. 1931. 11 x 15⅛″. 25 imprs.

Landscape Space #4. 1939. 10 x 12¾″. (4 colors.)

Titles marked by an asterisk indicate prints in the Collection of the Museum of Modern Art, gifts of Mrs. John D. Rockefeller, Jr.

Murals by Davis

New York, N. Y. Radio City Music Hall. Men's Lounge.
> *Men Without Women.* 1932. Oil on canvas, 11 x 17′.

Bloomington, Ind. Indiana University.
> *Swing Landscape.* 1938. Oil on canvas, 7 x 14′.
> Originally designed for the Williamsburgh Housing Project under the W.P.A.

New York, N. Y. Municipal Broadcasting System. Station WNYC. Studio B.
> Untitled. 1939. Oil on canvas, 7 x 11′.

Flushing, Long Island. New York World's Fair. Communications Building.
> *History of Communications.* 1939. 140 x 45′.

Bibliography

The arrangement is alphabetical, under the author's name, or under the title in the case of unsigned articles. Publications of museums are entered under the city in which the institution is located. Exhibition catalogs issued by private galleries and art organizations are listed under the name of the gallery or group. All material has been examined by the compiler, except item preceded by †.

ABBREVIATIONS Ag August, Ap April, bibl bibliography, D December, F February, il illustration(s), Ja January, Jy July, Mr March, My May, N November, no number, O October, p page(s), por portrait, S September, sec section, sup supplement(ary).

SAMPLE ENTRY for magazine article. RILEY, MAUDE. Stuart Davis exhibits his abstracted views. il Art Digest 17:7 F 1 1943.

EXPLANATION. An article by Maude Riley, entitled "Stuart Davis exhibits his abstracted views" is illustrated, and will be found in Art Digest, volume 17, page 7, the February 1, 1943 issue.

* Items so marked are in the Museum Library.

HANNAH B. MULLER

Writings by Davis

*1 ABSTRACT ART IN THE AMERICAN SCENE. il Parnassus 13:100-3 Mr 1941.

2 THE ABSTRACT IN MURAL ART. *In* United Scenic Artists' Association. Almanac. p20 1940-41.

3 ABSTRACTION. New York Times sec9 p7 Ag 20 1939.

*4 THE AMERICAN ARTIST NOW. Now (New York) lno1:7-11 Ag 1941.

5 AMERICAN ARTISTS AND THE "AMERICAN SCENE." New York World Telegram p14 My 4 1935.

*6 [AMERICAN ARTISTS' CONGRESS] Art Digest 10:25 Mr 15 1936.

*7 THE AMERICAN ARTISTS' CONGRESS. Art Front 2no8:8 D 1935.

*8 ART AND THE MASSES. Art Digest 14:13,34 O 1 1939.
> Summation of points at issue in New York Times controversy between abstract and nonobjectivist artists (bibl. 3, 67).

9 ART AT THE FAIR. Nation 149:112 Jy 22 1939.

*9a ART OF THE CITY. *In* Helena Rubinstein's New Art Center, New York. Masters of abstract art. p12-13 1942.

*10 THE ARTIST TODAY: THE STANDPOINT OF THE ARTISTS' UNION. American Magazine of Art 28:476-8, 506 Ag 1935.

*11 THE ARTISTS' CONGRESS AND AMERICAN ART. *In* American Artists' Congress. Second annual membership exhibition. p[2-5]. New York, 1938.

*12 CUBE ROOT. il (1 col) Art News 41:22-3,33-4 F 1 1943.

13 DAVIS ASKS A FREE ART. New York Times sec9 p12 Jy 7 1940.
   Further remarks, New York Times sec9 p7 Ag 18 1940.

*14 DAVIS' REJOINDER TO THOMAS BENTON. Art Digest 9:12-13,26 Ap 1 1935.
   Occasioned by Benton's reply to Davis' article (bibl. 26).

15 EXPLAINS HIS RESIGNATION FROM ARTISTS' CONGRESS. New York Times sec9 p9 Ap 14 1940.

16 FOREWORD TO EXHIBITION CATALOG: HANANIAH HARARI. New York, Mercury Galleries, 1939.

*17 FOREWORD to leaflet published by The Pinacotheca, New York, D 1941.

*18 INTRODUCTION. *In* Whitney Museum of American Art, New York. Abstract painting in America. p3-5 1935.

*   Reprinted in Art of Today 6no3:9-10 Ap 1935.
*   Reprinted in part in Homer Saint-Gaudens. The American artist and his times. p224-5 New York, Dodd, Mead, 1941.

*19 IS THERE A REVOLUTION IN THE ARTS? Town Meeting: Bulletin of America's Town Meeting of the Air 5no19:11-14 F 19 1940.

20 [LETTER OBJECTING TO JEWELL'S CRITICISM OF FEDERAL ART PROJECT EXHIBITION AT THE MUSEUM OF MODERN ART] New York Times sec10 p9 S 27 1936.

21 [LETTER ON MUNICIPAL ART CENTER] New York Sun p22 Ja 14 1935.

*22 [LETTER TO MCBRIDE ON FRENCH INFLUENCE IN DAVIS' PAINTINGS] Creative Art 6:sup34-5 F 1930.
   McBride's reply, Creative Art 6:sup 35 F 1930.

23 [LETTER TO MR. JEWELL DENYING ABSTRACTION OF PAINTING "ARBORETUM BY FLASH-BULB"] New York Times sec8 p5 S 27 1942.

*24 A MEDIUM OF 2 DIMENSIONS. Art Front 1no5:6 My 1935.

*25 THE "MODERN TREND" IN PAINTING. il Think 11no1:19-20,36 Ja 1945.

*26 THE NEW YORK AMERICAN SCENE IN ART. Art Front 1no3:6 F 1935.
   Reprinted in part and with comment in Art Digest 9no11:4,21 Mr 1 1935. Benton replies in Art Digest 9no12:20-1,25 Mr 15 1935; reprinted in Art Front 1no4:4,8 Ap 1935. For Davis' rejoinder, see bibl. 14.

27 A PAINTER OF CITY STREETS: AN ANALYSIS OF THE WORK OF GLENN COLEMAN. Shadowland 8no6:11,75 Ag 1923.

*28 PAINTINGS BY SALVADOR DALI, JULIEN LEVY GALLERY. Art Front 1no2:7 Ja 1935.

*29 PERSONAL STATEMENT. *In* David Porter Gallery, Washington, D.C. Personal statement: painting prophecy 1950. p[10] 1945.

30 [RESPONSE TO "BOMBSHELL" COMMUNICATION OF MR. KOOTZ] New York Times sec9 p9 O 12 1941.

*31 SELF-INTERVIEW. il (1 col) Creative Art 9:208-11 S 1931.

32 SHADOW. Harper's Bazaar 46:226-8 My 1912.

33 SHOW IS MODEL IN ORGANIZATION OF BIG DISPLAYS. New York Post p4WF Ap 29 1939.
   Comment on exhibition of contemporary American art at the World's Fair.

*34 SOME CHANCE! Art Front 1no7:4,7 N 1935.

35 WHAT ABOUT MODERN ART AND DEMOCRACY? Harper's Magazine 188:16-23 D 1943.

*36 WHY AN ARTISTS' CONGRESS? *In* First American Artists' Congress. p3-6 New York, 1936.
   See also bibl. 36a, 45, 53, 67, 70, 71.

Books, Articles, Catalogs

*36a AMERICAN ARTISTS GROUP. Stuart Davis. 64p il New York, 1945. (American artists group monographs).
   Text by Stuart Davis.

*37 ARTS CLUB OF CHICAGO. 3 contemporary Americans: Karl Zerbe, Stuart Davis, Ralston Crawford. 4p 1945.
   Exhibition catalog listing 13 paintings by Davis.

*38 [BIOGRAPHY] *In* Current Biography . . . 1940. p228-9 por New York, H. W. Wilson, 1940.

*39 BOSTON. INSTITUTE OF MODERN ART. Four modern American painters: Peter Blume . . . Stuart Davis . . . Marsden Hartley . . . Jacob Lawrence. 3p 1945.
   Exhibition catalog listing 13 paintings by Davis.

*40 BOSWELL, PEYTON. Painted jazz. Art Digest 17:3 F 15 1943.
   Exhibition, Downtown Gallery, New York.

†41 BOWDOIN, W. G. Modern work of Stuart Davis a Village show. New York Evening World D 13 1917.
   Exhibition, Sheridan Square Gallery, New York.

42 BURNETT, WHIT. "Egg beater" painter led American interpretive art. il New York Herald (Paris) Jy 7 1929.

43 BURROWS, CARLYLE. Stuart Davis . . . Downtown Gallery. New York Herald Tribune sec6 p5 F 7 1943.

44 CARY. ELIZABETH LUTHER. "Americans abroad." New York Times sec9 p12 O 13 1929.
Exhibition, Downtown Gallery, New York (with others).

*45 CINCINNATI MODERN ART SOCIETY. Marsden Hartley, Stuart Davis. 16p il 1941.
Exhibition catalog, listing 21 paintings and including bibliography. "Art in painting, by Stuart Davis," p7-8.

*46 COATES, ROBERT M. Davis, Hartley, and the River Seine. New Yorker 18:58 F 13 1943.
Exhibition, Downtown Gallery, New York.

47 CRILLON GALLERIES, PHILADELPHIA. Stuart Davis. 3p il 1931.
Exhibition catalog.

48 CRITICS LAUD YOUNG ARTIST. Newark Morning Ledger p3 Je 1 1918.
Exhibition, Ardsley Gallery, Brooklyn.

49 CROSS WORD PUZZLE MOTIF IN ART EXPRESSED ON CANVAS AT MUSEUM. Newark Evening News sup sec p11 F 9 1925.
Exhibition, Newark Museum and Public Library.

*50 DAVIS "AMERICAN SCENE." Art Digest 6:16 Mr 15 1932.
Exhibition, Downtown Gallery, New York.

*51 DAVIS TRANSLATES HIS ART INTO WORDS. il Art Digest 5:8 Ap 15 1931.
Exhibition, Downtown Gallery, New York. Includes quotation from Davis' introduction to catalog.

*52 DOWNTOWN GALLERY, NEW YORK. "The American scene" exhibition: recent paintings, New York and Gloucester . . . Stuart Davis. 3p il 1932.

*53 ——— Exhibition: Stuart Davis. 3p il 1931.
Exhibition catalog with introduction by Davis.

54 ——— Hotels and cafés, Stuart Davis. 5p il 1930.
Exhibition catalog.

*55 ——— Stuart Davis exhibition . . . recent paintings, oil and watercolor. 2p il 1934.
Exhibition catalog.

*56 ——— Stuart Davis: exhibition. 3p il 1943.
Exhibition catalog.

57 DU BOIS, GUY PÈNE. Stuart Davis. New York American p11 O 31 1910.
Exhibition Henri School of Art, New York.

*58 ——— Stuart Davis. Arts Weekly 1no3:48 Mr 26 1932.

*59 E., L. . . Stuart Davis. Art News 32:9 Ap 28 1934.
Exhibition, Downtown Gallery, New York.

*59a ESQUIRE'S ART INSTITUTE II. col il Esquire 24no3:68-9 S 1945.
Comments on Stuart Davis and his Garage Lights.

*60 GILBERT, MORRIS. Eggbeater artist defends credit to France for help given American painters. il por New York World Telegram p13 F 21 1940.

*61 GOODRICH, LLOYD. In the galleries. il The Arts 16:432 F 1930.
Exhibition, Downtown Gallery, New York.

*62 GORKY, ARSHELE. Stuart Davis. il Creative Art 9:212-17 S 1931.

63 HARRIS, RUTH GREEN. Stuart Davis. New York Times sec8 p13 Ja 26 1930.
Exhibition, Downtown Gallery, New York.

*64 HOT STILL-SCAPES FOR SIX COLORS—7TH AVE. STYLE. il Parnassus 12:6 D 1940.

*65 IMPRESSION OF THE NEW YORK WORLD'S FAIR PAINTED FOR HARPER'S BAZAAR BY STUART DAVIS. col il Harper's Bazaar 72:60-1 F 1939.

*66 JANIS, SIDNEY. Abstract & surrealist art in America. p50,53 il New York, Reynal & Hitchcock, 1944.

67 JEWELL, EDWARD ALDEN. Abstraction and music: newly installed WPA murals at Station WNYC raise anew some old questions. New York Times sec9 p7 Ag 6 1939.
Includes statements by Davis, amplified in bibl. 3.

68 ——— Davis tames a shrew. New York Times sec10 p18 Ap 19 1928.
Exhibition, Valentine Gallery, New York (with Glenn Coleman).

69 ——— Stuart Davis offers a penetrating survey of the American scene. New York Times p19 Mr 10 1932.
Exhibition, Downtown Gallery, New York.

70 JOHNSON, D. RHODES. Stuart Davis' paintings refute the silly notion that all modern art is "foreign." Jersey Journal p6 Jy 7 1941.
Includes statement by Davis.

*71 KLEIN, JEROME. Stuart Davis criticizes critic of abstract art. New York Post p24 F 26 1938.
Includes statement by Davis

*72 KOOTZ, SAMUEL M. New frontiers in American painting. p35,37-9 il New York, Hastings House, 1943.

73 MCBRIDE, HENRY. Stuart Davis comes to town. New York Sun p12 Ap 4 1931.
Exhibition, Downtown Gallery, New York.

74 McBRIDE, HENRY. Stuart Davis . . . Downtown Gallery. New York Sun p6 Mr 21 1932.

75 ———— Whitney Studio Club opens an exhibition. New York Sunday Herald sec3 p11 May 8 1921.

*76 NEW YORK. MUSEUM OF MODERN ART. Murals by American painters and photographers. p [22] il 1932.
    Exhibition catalog.

*77 ———— What is modern painting, by Alfred H. Barr, Jr. p4-5 il 1943. (Introductory series to the modern arts 2)

78 NEW YORK BY STUART DAVIS. New York Sun p16 Ap 28 1934.
    Exhibition, Downtown Gallery.

*79 O'CONNOR, JOHN, JR., Stuart Davis . . . awarded third honorable mention. il Carnegie Magazine 18no5:149-50 O 1944.

*80 PAUL, ELLIOT. Stuart Davis, American painter. il Transition no14:146-8 1928.

*81 PEARSON, RALPH M. Experiencing American pictures. p36-8 il New York and London, Harper, 1943.

*82 RILEY, MAUDE. Stuart Davis exhibits his abstracted views. il Art Digest 17:7 F 1 1943.
    Exhibition, Downtown Gallery, New York.

*83 SACARTOFF, ELIZABETH. Rockport, Mass., looks this way to Stuart Davis. il por PM p46 Ag 4 1940.

*84 SHELLEY, MELVIN GEER. Around the galleries. Creative Art 10:302 Ap 1932.
    Exhibition, Downtown Gallery, New York.

*85 STUART DAVIS . . . AT THE DOWNTOWN GALLERY. Art Digest 4:17 F 1 1930.

*86 STUART DAVIS AND ABSTRACTION. Art Digest 8:14 My 15 1934.
    Exhibition, Downtown Gallery, New York.

*87 STUART DAVIS, DOWNTOWN GALLERY. Art News 30:10 Mr 12 1932.

*88 STUART DAVIS, THE DIFFICULT. Art Digest 6:2 Ap 1 1932.
    Exhibition, Downtown Gallery, New York.

89 . . . STUART DAVIS . . . WHITNEY STUDIO CLUB GALLERIES. New York World p12 D 13 1926.

90 VALENTINE GALLERY, NEW YORK. Exhibition: paintings and water colors. 2p 1928.
    Exhibition catalog.

91 WHITNEY STUDIO CLUB, NEW YORK. Retrospective exhibition of paintings by Stuart Davis. 3p 1926.
    Exhibition catalog.

92 WHITNEY STUDIO GALLERIES, NEW YORK. Exhibition: water colors by Stuart Davis. 2p 1929.
    Exhibition catalog.

Index to Davis Quotations in Text

Three thousand copies of this book have been printed in October, 1945, for the Trustees of the Museum of Modern Art by the Plantin Press, New York. The color inserts have been printed by William E. Rudge's Sons, New York.

70832

THREE AMERICAN MODERNIST
PAINTERS.

DATE DUE
